BARRY JOHN'S WORLD OF RUGBY

BARRY JOHN'S

WORLD OF RUGBY

W. H. Allen / Christopher Davies

© 1978 W. H. Allen & Co. Ltd, and
Christopher Davies (Publishers) Ltd.

Published in 1978 by W. H. Allen & Co. Ltd.,
44 Hill Street, London W1X 8LB, in association with
Christopher Davies (Publishers) Ltd.,
52 Mansel Street, Swansea SA1 5EL

Printed in Wales by Salesbury Press Ltd., Swansea.

Photographs © Colorsport, London.

ISBN 0 491 02057 0

Introduction

Rugby is a game that is played and followed throughout the world, from Argentina to Japan, from Rumania to New Zealand, and it has an ambience all of its own.

The aim in compiling this volume is to reflect rugby's individuality, and to discover what the players, critics and fans have to say about the game. They look back at past seasons and the home International season, and forward to the coming championship and at the future of the game itself.

With changing rules, and new teams emerging, both local and national, Rugby is becoming a major spectator sport. But it was never more essential that the 'fun' element in the game was not overtaken by a ruthless and professional desire to win at all costs. Winning *is* important, but *how* one wins is of far greater importance — especially if rugby is to continue to attract and captivate world audiences.

This book captures this 'entertaining' aspect of the game and all the contributions to it attempt to show how essential that is.

B.J.

Contents

1 Where are England's goalkickers?

by JOHN REASON

England have learned in each of the last two seasons that winning the international championship now depends as heavily as it ever did on goalkicking. After the running rugby produced in those heady seasons of the early 'seventies — running produced partly by the major changes in the laws in 1970, and partly by the magnificent example set by the 1971 British Lions — the game in Europe has swung sharply back to a much more defensive and physical approach in which success is measured by the accuracy percentage of goalkickers. This is a bitter truth discovered by the 1977 British Lions in New Zealand.

For the second year in succession, England beat Scotland and Ireland and lost to France and Wales but they would have shared the international championship, and possibly won it outright, both in 1977 and in 1978 if they had what New Zealanders call 'a real gun goalkicker'. That one asset alone would have enabled them to beat France in 1977 and to beat Wales at Twickenham in 1978, for whom Phil Bennett won the match by kicking one more goal than England from three fewer chances.

Leaving aside the long-term implications behind this state of affairs — and ultimately, they are much more important and disturbing than the short-term consideration of who wins what — England did no more than achieve the respectability of four points out of eight and finish in the middle of the table

because they did not kick their goals. What is worse, their selection committee did not evaluate international Rugby at the moment and establish that goalkicking is the number one priority in team selection.

Having failed to do that, the selectors also failed to retain the goalkicker best equipped to give them their best possible return from chances offered in international matches. England made other fundamental selection errors, too, notably in the front and second rows of their pack at the end of the season, but it was in the matter of goalkicking that they failed most notably to grasp the essentials of team selection in 1977 and 1978. France, of course, made the same mistake. For thoroughly unworthy political reasons, they left Jean-Pierre Romeu out of their team and chose to play the whole season without either a goalkicker or a fly-half. France had more good players than anyone else, and in terms of pressure and position and length of periods of domination, they had the better of every match they played, but they lost the championship because they did not kick their goals.

Ray McLoughlin, the former Irish and British Lions prop, is possibly the most penetrating intellect produced by British Rugby in the last twenty years, and he is in no doubt at all that the name of the game at international level at the moment is goalkicking. Not only does he believe that the selection of goalkickers and back-up goalkickers is the essence of

9

match-planning, but he also believes that it is just as important to pick players who will not concede penalty kicks within range of goal. For that reason, he thinks that England's greatest achievement last season was in playing the Calcutta Cup match against Scotland at Murrayfield without conceding one penalty kick in their half of the field. It is impossible to refute McLoughlin's arguments, particularly if you compile a statistical breakdown of every piece of play in every international match. (This suggests, incidentally, that the most constructive step the International Rugby Football Board could take at the moment would be to introduce a two-year experiment in which no kicks at goal were allowed at all, except for foul play, persistent infringement, or after a try has been scored.)

As things stand, however, our international Rugby has reached the point where the goalkicker is so dominant that if we are logical, we should treat him just as they do in American football, and bring him on the field just to take kicks at goal, if necessary in a wheel-chair! It is for this reason that England's decision to play their last three matches last season without Alan Old, who was their only goalkicker with any real pretentions at international level, was so ill-advised.

In the last ten years, England have had four goalkickers of international class, but they only established two of them as international Rugby players. The four were Bob Hiller, George Cole, Alan Old

Right:
England's decision to omit Old was ill-advised.

No place for Romeu in the French team.

and the late Sam Doble. Of those, Cole did not play for England at all, and although Doble won a match for England against South Africa at Ellis Park, he was never really an established international. The only two who have had a run in the England team are Hiller and Old.

In 1977, Old spent the entire international season as a reserve, but last season, as Martin Cooper lost a bit of form, it seemed as if Old would play the whole season for England. His goal-kicking took Yorkshire to the semi-finals of the county championship and his partnership at half-back with Malcolm Young had much to do with the success of the North of England team that won the Rugby Union's newly in-augurated divisional championship.

It is true that for almost the whole of his first-class career, Alan Old's play at fly-half has suffered from the fact that he has played his week-by-week Rugby for less than first-class clubs like Middles-brough and Sheffield. As 'Chalky' White, Leicester's sagacious coach says, "Too many of England's best players do not have to play their best football often enough for their own good," and many

England's captain, Beaumont, is tackled by Biggar (Scotland).

players in the North of England like Alan Old are in that situation. (Incidentally, Billy Beaumont, the England captain, is another.) But Old showed with the Lions in South Africa in 1974 what he could do if he had regular experience of top-class · football and although he has not been able to reach his own personal peak since, through circumstances of his residence, he has still been England's best equipped goal-kicker since the retirement of Bob Hiller.

Old was chosen for England's first match last season, against France in Paris, but the somehow inevitable partnership of Young and Old at half-back lasted only one game. Old was then dropped and he understandably declined to be mucked about any more and asked to be excused selection as a reserve for the rest of the season. In his place, England chose John Horton and almost certainly lost the chance of winning the Triple Crown and sharing the championship as a result.

This is no criticism of Horton as a fly-half, but the fact is that the goalkicking requirement over-rides all others. I remember Martin Cooper feeling aggrieved the previous season when his place as a fly-half was in jeopardy because of England's goalkicking failures elsewhere, but with the game as it is framed at the moment, this has to be. In

Paul Dodge improved England's midfield.

Burton in action against France.

any case, the margins between Alan Old and John Horton as fly-halves are minimal — not more than two or three per cent — whereas the goalkicking consideration is paramount.

With John Horton and Paul Dodge in midfield, England's back play *did* improve in their last two matches against Scotland and Ireland, but the fact is that a goalkicker could have won England their game against Wales, and that was the decisive match of their season.

Alastair Hignell kicked at goal for England against Wales, as he did against France the year before, and although I regard him as second only to J. P. R. Williams in the essentials of full-back play — catching, tackling, positioning and football sense — I have never regarded him as an international class

goalkicker. Even so, he had more pretensions than those who succeeded him, because when he withdrew from England's match against Scotland because of injury, England chose to play their last two matches without a practising goalkicker at all! This was like entering a Grand Prix race without a motor-car. The fact that England won those two games should deceive no one as to the appalling risk they took.

This, then, was England's biggest shortcoming, and their biggest mistake, and there are no signs that it will be rectified next season. The sad thing is that when England make mistakes in selection, they do it in such a way as to burn their boats entirely in the position concerned, and as often as not, they destroy the fleet in an absolutely crucial part of the game. They have done it with

Alan Old and their goalkicking. They have done it with Mickey Burton in their front row. They have also done it with Nigel Horton as a Number Four lineout jumper. As these are probably three of the four keys to a successful team, one can only wonder at the approach to strategic planning.

The decision to drop Nigel Horton was almost beyond belief. In 25 years of writing about Rugby football, I have never heard such undiluted incredulity from the top players in the game as that expressed when they heard the news. Days afterwards, they were still shaking their heads. No one was more surprised than Maurice Colclough, who was chosen to replace Horton. He was the first to admit that he was not even in Horton's league as a lineout forward, and there was instant proof of this when England played Scotland and found themselves scratching for possession.

This decision, and the persistent refusal to choose Fran Cotton at loose head with Mickey Burton at tight head precipitated Burton's retirement and left England's pack in worse shape than it had been for three seasons. Even Ireland, who had been pushed from pillar to post by everyone in sight because of their dire lack of a tight head, found them-

Nigel Horton tries to break through the Welsh line.

selves winning plus marks in the scrummage when they arrived at Twickenham. At first, they could not believe it, but as the match wore on, and the Irish forwards assured themselves that they were not really dreaming, they were encouraged by events in the scrummage to lift their game to the point where they were really competing as a pack. This was a remarkable achievement considering that, in the same way that France had chosen to play without a fly-half and goalkicker, Ireland played the whole season without a big man jumping in the middle of the lineout.

The danger from England's point of view, of course, is that as they beat both Ireland and Scotland, the selectors will probably approach next season either unaware of the fact that the senior pro's in their pack are deeply disturbed by the decline in the forward performance or determined to stick their heads in the sand and pretend that the decline is a figment of the imagination.

The problems are not likely to be recognised, much less resolved, because England's tight forward selections have been fundamentally unsound since the present selection committee was

17

Squires scores against Scotland.

Left:
Cotton was never chosen as loose head.

formed. Unfortunately, neither John Pullin nor 'Stack' Stevens were able to accept invitations to become selectors because they wanted to go on playing (though why that should have disqualified them, I do not know) and so the present England selection committee have no tight forwards among them who have had playing contact with the modern game. Even worse, they have members of the committee — splendid men when evaluating their own specialist areas of the game — who are actively and vociferously pulling the boat in the wrong direction as far as the tight forwards are concerned.

The pity is that these mistakes are all so avoidable. All the selectors have to do is take John Pullin out to lunch a couple of times in the season, and take his advice. He is one of the most experienced hookers in the world and he is certainly the most knowledgeable man about hookers and props in England.

Better still, the selectors should recall Pullin as England's reserve hooker to Peter Wheeler. Pullin intends to go on playing, and no one is nearly as well qualified as he is to go on the field to hook in a crucial situation. By having him in their squad, the selectors would have a fund of experience and

19

thoroughly up-to-date knowledge at their disposal. So he is a former England captain! So what! No other hooker has come within sight of Pullin and Wheeler as technicians capable of filling that highly specialised position for England, and in the meantime, England have put themselves in some peril of giving a cap or caps to players who are not yet anywhere near good enough. The age factor ought not to come into it. After all, Stan Hodgson had not even begun his international career for England at Pullin's present age, and in any case, I have always believed that the traditional principle established by the Springboks and All Blacks in these matters was the right one. Their view was that once a player, particularly a forward, had established that he was of genuine Springbok or All Black class, he stayed in the team as a member of a proud and exclusive élite until either he was beaten out of sight by a young rival, or he decided to retire, or he dropped dead! John Pullin has come nowhere near any of those contingencies just yet.

The England 'B' tour of Rumania at the end of last season certainly revealed no solutions to England's problems. Tony Bond did enough to suggest that he will go into next season's trials as favourite to play alongside Paul Dodge in the centre, but Bob Demming, who was England's best attacking runner in Rumania, celebrated his 29th birthday on tour and although it is true that Jim Roberts played some fine Rugby for England at a similar age, the chances are that Demming's best years are behind him.

John Fidler, the Gloucester lock, also played well, but he is now 30. Fidler is one of those forwards who should have picked up the occasional cap when Chris Ralston or Nigel Horton were either injured or not available, but he missed

out. Inferior players were capped instead.

In other positions, England made no progress. Not that they could be expected to. After all, England have tried some pretty comprehensive permutations in their attempts to hit the international jackpot in the last ten years. There are at least seven England international fly-halves who are still playing Rugby, and similarly there are seven England full-backs and six England scrum-halves. As full internationals could not be chosen for the 'B' team, that meant that England's choices in those positions for Rumania rated eight, eight and seven respectively. Inevitably, this restricted England's first venture into 'B' team Rugby either to sound club players or to young hopefuls who are not likely to mature for two or three seasons. This is one of the penalties of having an unsettled full international team for so long.

As it turned out, the England 'B' tour of Rumania was not productive from any point of view. In retrospect, it was a mistake for England not to play the full Rumanian international team, because at the end of the tour, England were no wiser about the real strength of Rumanian Rugby than they were at the beginning. I should be surprised, however, if the Rugby Football Union show any great enthusiasm about extending their playing contacts with the countries in Eastern Europe. For one thing, the British fixture list is too crowded, and for another, the state apparatus in Eastern Europe is so suffocating and so pervasive that it produces an atmosphere which is not our scene at all. There is intense local enthusiasm to expand their Rugby horizons, the hospitality could not have been more lavish and I personally met some marvellous Rugby men, but I returned absolutely convinced that the traditionally conserva-

Left:
Wheeler — England's hooker.

21

Slemen tackled.

tive instinct of British Rugby administrators to keep on opposite sides of the fence is the right one.

I quoted an amusing remark by Steve Boyle, and it was quoted back from *The Daily Telegraph* with such gravity that apparently, even the British Embassy in Bucharest began to tut-tut. Well, once we lose our sense of humour about Rugby football, and once we feel that it would be better not to share a laugh for fear of up-setting a political dictatorship, we might as well all go home. I personally feel sad for Rumania, and Rumanian Rugby. Left to their own Latin devices, the place would be swinging like the South of France in less than six months, but as things are, I agree with your man R. Kipling, who must have had Rugby football in mind when he said, "East is East and West is West, and never the 'twain shall meet."

2 2078/79?

MAX BOYCE

'Who'll be here in a hundred years?'
Pwy fydd yma 'mhen can mlynedd — is
the recurring refrain in a much-loved
popular song chorussed in Welsh pubs
and chapels. I began by calling it a hymn,
but it's actually an old Sankey & Moody
song translated by a great Welsh
hymnologist. You'd understand my
mistake if you'd heard it sung as often as
I have and accorded the same reverence
as our best-loved terrace hymn, Bread of
Heaven.

In the part of Wales where I was born
and bred, Rugby Football stirs similar
emotions in the people as does that
lovely old favourite. It follows then
naturally for me to ask of our National
Game "Pwy fydd yma 'mhen can
mlynedd?" Who will inspire the song-
writer in the season 2078-9, who will
sharpen the pencil of a Gren, who will
fill the kiln of a John Hughes, who will
incur the wrath of a T. P. Maclean or
befriend a J.B.G.?

When I first began to ponder over the
question, my mind went back to a dark
winter's night, with the wind blowing up
from the sea, when an old man was
washed ashore at Swansea Bay, hanging
on to a piece of driftwood he'd fashioned
crudely into a boat. His eyes sunk deep
into his skull, his skin pulled tight over
his bones, he had lived on raw fish and
sea bird eggs for longer than he could
remember. The notches on his make-
shift sail told of the years of drifting with
ever-changing winds and tides. The
ship-wrecked, weather-beaten old man
stumbled into the arms of some local
fishermen.

"Tell me," he croaked, as they
wrapped him in a warm blanket to rush
him to Singleton Hospital.

"Tell me, for I have not spoken to
another soul for so long. Tell me all that
has happened while I have been at sea.
Has man succeeded in his attempts to
put a man into space? Has the cross-
channel tunnel been completed? Has
man finally climbed Everest?"

We gladly answered all his questions
and then impressed on him the urgency
of his condition and the need to get him
to hospital.

"One last question," he begged. "One
last question: tell me — has Charlie
Faulkner retired yet?"

Charlie Faulkner, good old Charlie,
second to none. What an inspiration he
has been, one who has stolen a few tight
heads against time — even he *perhaps*
will have to give way in the year 2078.

What then of the future? I decided the
man to ask was the project engineer in
the Outside-Half Factory — Dai
Tolerance.

I rang him up and arranged for a
factory visit. I was met by the Works
Manager who had great delight in
showing me around and explaining the
many Technological advances that had
been made since my last visit. We went
first to the Recovery Department where
outside-halves that had become
ineffective were being re-cycled and
treated. The most common fault, he ex-

plained, was malfunction of the judgement diaphragm which resulted in players kicking when in fact they should have passed.

The treatment was brilliant in its conception and yet so simple. It required the player under test to sit in a booth where assimilated conditions, on film, were shown to him on a screen, complete with sound track of the crowd noises. When the film was shown, he was encouraged to press a 'Green Button' marked PASS, if he saw fit, or a 'Red Button' marked KICK should he decide otherwise. If, according to the computor, he chose wrong, an electric impulse would energise a solenoid 'S1' and a long thin stainless steel spike, situated beneath the player under test, would be driven into the region of his buttocks. The back contact on the spike would then de-energise 'S1' and the cycle would start all over again.

This method had apparently been quite successful until one morning a contact stuck in and the spike operated twenty-five times before the machine operator could shut it off. Needless to say, the design engineer had to be called in and the spike, which was badly bent, replaced. The player apparently never fully recovered and is now playing somewhere in Surrey.

The system has, so I was told, one other drawback. When one of the outside-halves, so treated and passed by inspection, played in his first match, and was instructed by his captain to kick at every opportunity because of the dreadful handling conitions, he replied, "Only if you switch the 'Spike' off."

Much impressed, we left recovery and proceeded through 'Export' and 'Arms and Legs' to the new section of the factory where the strictest security precautions were in operation.

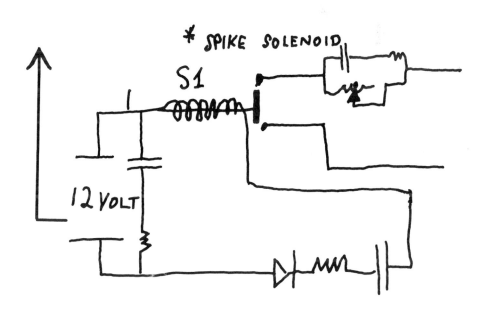

We were interrogated and searched, then blindfolded and taken through, what seemed to be endless twisting passageways, to a section of the plant known as 'F.23'. We were then screened and held under the strictest surveillance and searched again. Only then were we shown the latest break-through which, according to the designer, was the most exciting and revolutionary conception since the BENNY (The Swivel Side-step Joint). All around me I was aware of this strange hum. All the works staff were dressed in long black rubber suits with rubber gloves and special breathing apparatus.

It was then I saw them for the first time the 'Flair Vats'. I couldn't believe my eyes. There were these long

IN THE INTERESTS OF NATIONAL SECURITY THIS SECTION OF THE ARTICLE HAS BEEN DELETED TO COMPLY WITH THE OFFICIAL SECRETS ACT 1956. WE REGRET ANY INCONVENIENCE CAUSED TO THE READERS.

ED.

It took me several minutes to recover from my initial shock and I was glad when Idwal suggested a cup of tea in his office.

Fully recovered, we now spoke excitedly about the future of Welsh Rugby and how the only thing that bothered him was the 'win at all costs' attitude and the thuggery that had entered the game at all levels. I agreed and quoted one of my songs from the Album *I Was There,*

If we lose it matters not
For there the sadness ends
For defeats ne'r counted as a loss
If it be the gain of friends

I stressed to him that the quality Rugby Union had was the ability to foster Friendship and Kinship and how this was more important than winning or losing. He nodded in agreement. I was glad to see he felt as I did, but then as I left his office I saw displayed above his office door a plaque in a glass case on which was written:

When it comes for the one great
    scorer
to mark against your name,
He'll not ask how you played the game
But whether you beat England.

I left his office slightly dismayed at his attitude but knowing the future of Welsh Rugby was in good hands and with the knowledge after visiting 'F.23', —
Pwy fydd yma 'mhen can mlynedd?

3 The Gospel according to St. Noel

JOHN O'SHEA

The Gospel according to St. Noel of Cork was preached throughout the rugby speaking areas of Ireland during the season just past, with limited, if spectacular results.

Noel Murphy's arrival at the seat of real power in Irish rugby reminded one of the welcome which greeted De Gaulle when he liberated Paris at the end of the War.

Words such as 'renaissance' ... 'revival' ... 'resurgence' were being thrown about by people, whose task it was to preview the international championship.

Murphy had a legion of admirers. He advocated a concept of the game, based on determination and a will to succeed. His brief for the game was basic, tinged with a Cork shrewdness. Tactics would be kept to a minimum, but every player was expected to play as if his very life rested on the result.

For many it seemed that Irish rugby was poised to enter a new era: an era where victory and euphoria would replace gloom and humiliating defeat.

But not for the first time ambition failed to be matched by the requisite degree of skill needed to survive and conquer at this stratum of rugby.

One match only was won, and this, due entirely to a quite astonishing decision by Scottish captain Douglas Morgan. It was however an improvement on the points drought of the previous season.

Significantly the approach adopted by Ireland was refreshing. The days of fear and caution were banished, and instead we watched a team, which was for the bulk of the season, imbued with confidence in its ability to give battle against sides, who on paper at any event looked infinitely superior.

The motivation which Murphy engendered was to a large extent responsible for a Herculean performance against the French in Paris. It was present also in that fortuitous win over Scotland and for a time during the encounter with Wales.

Against England, however, in their final outing, Ireland played like a team who knew that they lacked the technical expertise to down moderate rivals: Murphy's influence had worn off.

Ireland gained two points because they were deserving no more than that. The side contained two deep-rooted weaknesses, which gave their opposition an overwhelming advantage.

Firstly, our line-out work was quite pathetic. Moss Keane, alone, seemed capable of out-leaping rivals out of touch. The second flaw was even more serious.

Decreeing that the Irish backs were brought into play at every opportunity, Murphy saw in new cap Tony Ward a man to articulate his philosophy. This Ward did, but a lack of flair and inventiveness in midfield made try-scoring a most hazardous task.

Full-back Tony Ensor, regrettably no longer available for international selection, was starved, despite his penchant

Moss Keane alone seemed capable of out-leaping rivals.

Left:
Morgan's astonishing decision gave Ireland her only win.

for creating likely scoring possibilities, and the speedy Freddy McLennan on the left-wing did not get the service he deserved.

These players, along with Mike Gibson, who operated on the right wing posed threats whenever in possession, but the side was too often dispossessed in midfield.

There's no doubt that the performance by the Irish selectors followed more logical guidelines than their immediate predecessors. Yet this group too were guilty of some poor and ill-judged workmanship.

Having lost Donal Spring after the opening international, they elected to use a back-row forward, Harry Steele, as Keane's lock partner. Fine forward though he is, Steele's qualities were not suited to the second-row.

They erred too in not altering the mid-field of Paul McNaughton and Alastair McKibbin: players solid in defence, yet stereotype in attack.

There was hardly universal agreement either that John Moloney should hold down the scrum-half berth for the four internationals. Johnny was an inspiring captain, but his short pass gave Ward little scope to express himself in an attacking vein.

Noel Murphy and his colleagues could have called upon the Trinity player, Mike Gibson — a noted line-out expert, but they decided, wrongly in my oppinion, that his unorthodoxy would unsettle the side. This observer is convinced, that had the 6ft. 6inch Gibson been used, our results would have been appreciably better.

Centres of skill and creativity were not thick on the ground in Ireland last season. Again we had two or three, notably David Roche and Moss Finn, who might have been tried with profit.

While Douglas Morgan's much publicised gesture enabled Ireland to snatch a three point win (12-9) over Scotland, the most pleasing aspect of this display was the performance of our pack. Here, the Irish forwards, for the first time in years, contravened Union regulations and ran with the ball. Four times the

Irish pack shed the shackles which had hitherto laced them to their menial stations and indulged in exhilarating and havoc-creating bouts of inter-passing.

A second bonus for Irish fans was the level of commitment shown. Men were toppled with full-blooded tackles in a way which convinced the onlooker that a seat in the electric chair was the punishment for an error in judgment.

The battle at the Parc des Princes (lost 9-10) was a triumph for Tony Ward and the Irish pack. In conditions more suited to ice-skating, Ward proved that sheer class can never be obliterated. Every-thing he touched turned to gold. His most valuable contribution was his three penalty goals, but it was his verve and poise which created the deepest impression.

Lodged in permanent residence in the memory is an incident, early in the game, when the cocky fly-half stepped inside an attempted tackle from Rives. Seconds later he repeated the act.

Emmet O'Rafferty did not of course play in the Parc des Princes that afternoon ... but there are thousands of French supporters who will swear they saw him in action.

The most pleasing aspect of Irish play was the pack.

32

A leg injury forced O'Rafferty out of the game on the morning of the game, but the news that he had been replaced by Steele was not passed on to the spectators. They were left in blissful ignorance of the change as they broused through their match programme.

In fact I met an Englishman after the game who commented that he felt Emmet had made a useful début.

Never more than in the clash with Wales at Lansdowne Road were the twin shortcomings of sloppy line-out work and a dearth of midfield flair more exposed. How we longed for a switch which would have transferred the creative Gibson from the isolation of the wing into the heart of the attack.

Wales, having forged ahead 13-3, mainly through the accurate right boot of Steve Fenwick, relaxed their grip for a period, before emerging comprehensive winners (20-16). In truth, the four points separating the sides was hardly an accurate commentary on proceedings.

Gibson, that most gifted of all Irish rugby players, had reason to celebrate the encounter, for he had finally etched his name on the record books as the most capped player in the history of the code: a fitting tribute to his standard over a fourteen year period.

Gibson's outings in the green have been against: England (15), Scotland

The Irish pack on the break against Scotland.

Slattery 'gives'
instructions to
McKinney.

Left:
Ward in action against
England.

(13), Wales (14), France (15), Australia (4), New Zealand (2), South Africa (2) and President's XV (1).

And the news that he has his sights trained on the 100th cap will be greeted by the lighting of bonfires in every parish in the country.

If the Irish reached the zenith of their powers in Paris, they slumped to the nadir of ineffectiveness against the English at Twickenham. I recall turning to a colleague, Paul McWeeney, at the interval and enquiring if either of us had ever witnessed such a dismal performance from an Irish side.

Gone was the urgency of previous showings and in its place, a lethargy and *ennui* pervaded the entire side. England fashioned a well-taken try, scored by Mike Slemen, and this was the sole abiding memory of the defeat (9-15).

There was little for the fan to enthuse about during the interprovincial series, which finished inconclusively, with three provinces, Munster, Ulster and Leinster sharing top spot on six points.

Connacht, as has been their station for decades, propped up the group.

A piece of bravery, when he dived at the feet of Minster flanker, Colm Tucker, cost Mike Gibson his chance of collecting a cap against Scotland. The N.I.F.C. man sustained a hairline fracture of the shoulder and was ruled out for several weeks.

International winger Freddy McLennan, so harshly treated by the Irish selectors in recent seasons, was unquestionably the most effective three-quarter in the series, and his three trials were all spectacular efforts.

Perhaps the injection, by the Northern Bank (employers of Bill McBride) of £36,000 over the next three years, will breathe some life into a championship which is most definitely in need of a fillip.

Inevitably the prodigious scoring feats of Tony Ward attracted attention from the Rugby League moguls, one of whom is reputed to have been prepared to part with £16,000 for a piece of paper bearing the signature of the Garryowen fly-half.

But Tony would not countenance such a move. "I get too much enjoyment from playing the game for fun," he stated at the time.

Apart from equalling the record for the number of points scored by one individual in the championships (38 points), Ward came close to the magical 300 points mark for his tally at club level. He was responsible for 282 points, made up of 5 tries, 64 penalties, 4 drop-goals and 29 conversions.

The season was notable, too, for the fact that we might well have witnessed the last 'Colours' match to be staged at Lansdowne Road.

Because of a brawl which erupted minutes after the start of the annual U.C.D./Trinity confrontation, and which saw one player being ordered for a quick shower, the I.R.F.U. imposed an indefinite ban on future 'Colours' games being held at Headquarters.

On the club front, Corinthians, alone managed a League and Cup double. They had no peers in Connacht. Wanderers were somewhat surprising winners of the Leinster Senior Cup, downing a vaunted U.C.D. side in the decider. St. Marys' consistency enabled them to take the League title.

Garryowen contested both the Munster League and Cup finals, but lost out to Shannon (Cup) and U.C.C. (League).

Bill McBride was a power in Ballymena's Ulster Senior League triumph, while it was C.I.Y.M.S.'s turn to succeed in the Cup.

We had the odd sight during the Leinster Cup semi-final between U.C.D. and Blackrock College of seeing Willie Duggan occupying a seat on the 'Rock' bench throughout. The Lions No. 8 was deemed fit enough for stand-by duty because of an ankle injury.

Mention of the Lions reminds us of Moss Keane's reply to the T.V. question posed by Nigel Starmer-Smith. "What was the highlight of the tour from your viewpoint?" "When I heard from home that Kerry had beaten Cork in the Munster final," said the bold Moss.

Any wonder the interview was not beamed.

Right:
Duggan wins a line-out against England.

4 The changing face of Rugby

DAI HAYWARD

"You stand there, third from the front. That boy throwing the ball into the line-out is the wing threequarter. You try to catch it and give it to him standing there—he's the scrum half." This started and finished the only coaching session I ever had. In the tradition of the time — and I suspect today — the biggest boys in the class were always second-row forwards, the smallest played scrum-half and the fastest on the wings. The fattest always played prop-forward and the rest played in the positions that were dependant upon whether their current hero was Haydn Tanner, Billy Cleaver, Bleddyn Williams or Ken Jones.

After my first and only coaching session, I had many pieces of advice, many priceless and some ludicrous, but I never had another coaching session. There was an obvious need for Team coaching in the Cardiff sides that I played for and an even more obvious need in the Welsh teams that I played for. At Club level the mere fact that we played together every week, ironed out some of the faults, and fifteen individuals eventually started to blend into a team — but the Welsh XV, stayed exactly what it was — fifteen individuals. Albeit, very talented individuals, who gave everything they had in terms of ability and endeavour, but apart from the very basic and obvious moves — rarely achieved anything in the combined sense beyond contributing their own particular flashes of talent. At all levels of the game every-

one had his own responsibilities and generally stuck rigidly to them, which led to some incredible situations, but which were accepted by and large throughout the game. For example, a hooker's job was to win the ball in the set scrum. As long as he did that, and won the odd strike against the head, he wasn't required to do anything else, which probably explains why hookers went on for ever and were nearly always the oldest men in the side. (Discounting the present incumbents, Cardiff have had barely a half a dozen hookers in the last thirty years). Prop-forwards had two jobs, to help the hooker to strike for the ball, and to invent incredible tales of fantasy in case he lost it. Since they had no other responsibilities, and since they excluded all others from their highly technical conversations, they inevitably became introverted about their rôle. This resulted in the situation where the front row played one game and the rest of the team played another. It didn't really matter to them what the score read in the Football Echo — if they had taken two against the head — they had won.

Second-row forwards (Locks to the younger element) were there to push in the scrum and jump in the line-out, and very occasionally to kick goals. Open-side wing forwards and blind-side wing forwards were there to terrorise the outside and the inside halves respectively, and to do all the running for the front-five, in this they were aided by the lock-forward or No. 8. Scrum-halves were there to scream abuse at everyone in the pack when they didn't give him the ball, or, when they did, in a sloppy manner. His job was to protect the outside half and only give him the very best of service. Since outside-halves had all the say and only accepted perfect possession, this left the inside-half with many problems. Usually these were insoluble and so they didn't live long. Those that did became Welsh Internationals. Outside-halves were undoubtedly the darlings of the team, the selectors and the crowds. They were not expected to tackle or fall on the ball — the open-side wing forward did this for them. If they could catch the ball and make two clean breaks a match they had done their job. It didn't really matter if they couldn't kick or pass, because everyone was there to see them running with the ball. They were quite successful at this — but it would be rather more surprising if they weren't, since the only men delegated to stop them were the opposition open-sides. Since the average fly-half had eight men in his own pack dedicated to preventing this happening, and since his own scrum-half was buried more times than Houdini in his efforts to supply him with a good ball, he had most things going for him.

The threequarter line were there to capitalise on the breaks of the outside-half. If he could pass all was well — if he couldn't, they usually transferred to another club.

After the Welsh Team were soundly beaten by the South Africans in Durban in 1964, Wales decided to change all this and join Division One by setting up a coaching scheme. Thanks to the uncompromising ability and flair of Ray Williams, and a succession of good men as National Coaches, Wales at Club and National level took full advantage of the new laws, and a new and glorious episode began for Welsh Rugby. A series of wonderful teams containing wonderful players, playing wonderful rugby football. But now a pause for thought. Were we lucky to be organised at a time when there was great scope for innovation because of the significant changes in the laws? Would we have achieved as much anyway (because over the decade we churned out a dozen or more World Class players, possibly a half a dozen or so of whom, will rank the greatest) were it not for formal coaching? Or is it our club and coaching system, so geared that it will go on indefinitely churning out glittering gems from the Mother Lode of Welsh Talent.

I think that the truth lies not in the answer to any one of these questions, but is to be found in the gem of truth that lies in each of them — when they are put together as a whole.

Yes, we were probably lucky in that we decided to organise our talent at a time when the laws changed in favour of attacking Rugby played with flair. Yes, we were lucky to have such great players available to capitalise on this ground work, and yes, most of these players *were* the product of the first flush of Welsh Coaching. But then again, if coaching and organisation had existed for the Welsh Teams of the Haydn Tanner, Cliff Morgan, Bleddyn Williams era, what might they have achieved? It is the last question that causes the frowns, and poses the warning? We will always, one prays, produce more than our share of Rugby genius — but will it be allowed to flourish and reach its full fruits in the benign air of enlightened coaching, or will it wither in the freezing straight jacket of blind rugby dogma? I once saw a team with plenty of good forwards, and a back line that contained Gareth Edwards, Barry John, Gerald Davies, D. Ken Jones, Keri Jones and Maurice Richards, play ten man rugby against an unkown English club team. I could not believe what I was seeing — the situation screamed for adventurous running rugby. Years later I questioned Barry about that game, and he replied that by the time he followed instructions about what to do in certain situations, in various parts of the field, and by the time they had done all the rehearsed moves with the back row and the centres, there were only about five minutes left of the game to do his own thing and he didn't get the ball in that time. Fortunately, like most of the others, he had the character to do his own thing occasionally and coaches were new on the scene. It is impossible to go back to the days, when I was back-handed across the ear by an irate prop because I was pushing too hard and spoiling his balance. In my already ringing ears rang the unforgettable words, "You do my running and I'll do your bloody pushing." Before it dawned on me that rugby football could accommodate all types and was really a fun game, well not as serious as Paschendale or the Somme, I took the same prop to task for smoking whilst I was doing my strenuous pre-match work-out. "Look Boyo," came the reply, as he watched another smoke ring disappearing into the haze of wintergreen, "You warm up your way and I'll warm up mine." While it is impossible, and undesirable, to go back to the disorganised individuality of the past, may I make a plea for consideration of the individual? To all coaches, I say, nurture your talented individual, bear with his whims, suffer, for a while, small indisciplines but work at him until you can safely build a part of your game around him then show him the results for us all to marvel. Without *talent* you are lost — and so is every international team. By all means aim to emulate Ray Prosser's Pontypool Packs. I am not saying they are built without talent, but the pack is one area where rigid discipline and, the dedicated determination of all eight to go the same way together, pays handsome dividends. A pack like that creates the ball, the space and the opportunity for potential players of flair to prosper — if given the chance. There lies the rub. Winning matters, and running Rugby entails taking risks, but if it is any consolation, the most successful sides in Wales in the decade we have been considering have been Bridgend, Llanelli, London Welsh and Cardiff — all of them at some time have carried the banner of adventurous running Rugby Football. The mere fact that they have consistently practised running and handling in their games means that they reduce the number of errors. And look at the quality players, not to mention the odd genius that those clubs have thrown up in the process. As a consequence, Welsh International back play has consistently won matches and thrilled millions. By and large, they don't look surprised to get the ball in their hands, and they move with purpose and imagination, which cannot be said of some of the embarrassingly clumsy attempts seen by a few of their opponents. Having made a plea for the individual to the coaches, may I also be allowed to make a plea for all the players to everybody — coaches, selectors, club committees, supporters and the press? Remember, they are supposed to be playing for fun. They have jobs, families and a life to live outside of Rugby Football. The demands made at the top these days encroaches upon the time available for the wife and kids, the home and close friends. Don't encroach further by creating even more fixtures, and don't think they are being arrogant if they don't come to your party or can't open your Church Fête. The media have tended to make the stars of Rugby available to everybody — and coaches tend to become ever-more demanding — so do Tours and fixtures. My generation got a lot of fun out of Rugby — don't kill the fun — or this generation will get a lot less out of Rugby Football than I did — and they will have put in infinitely more.

5 Changes in the French camp

TONY LEWIS

France had won the Grand Slam in 1977 with an overpowering demonstration of strength in the forwards and shrewdness at half-back. Aguirre, their full-back, had grown more confident by the game and he had made the position his own. What more then could their national selectors wish as they made their plans for the 1978 season? Surely there was little reason for change.

The first accident was a large black fly in the ointment; the New Zealanders, on a short tour, defeated France. The usual incriminations of individuals followed and Jacques Fouroux, the French captain, a man not taken to endure criticism without shouting out a defence, suddenly announced his retirement from rugby football. You can squander all sorts of guesses on how intrigue behind the scenes ignited the explosion, but why bother? It is history now; the 'little general' was gone in a huff and a puff, and the Selectors had to find a leader and a scrum-half.

Jean-Pierre Bastiat of Dax was the obvious captain. As Number Eight he was well placed to view the play and influence the tactical lead, but who was to provide that lead from half-back?

Fouroux's play had been very skilfully shaped to the strength of his pack with kicks into the box, and darting breaks close to the set-pieces. However, it had not been popular with many of the French officials. Where is our traditional flair for passing? Why do we not see more of our wings than our wing-forwards? Those were the sort of questions asked.

Also, throughout 1977, their Grand Slam year, the French backs had been poor finishers of movements. So often the centres Bertranne and Sangali were guilty of delaying passes too long, failing to profit by the overlaps set up by Aguirre and poor passing resulted in the loss of simple tries.

So, as January approached, there was a lack of satisfaction in the French camp, and instead of sensibly refusing to tinker with an experienced machine which would surely roll effectively forward again, they sought to do more than just win. They made plans to use the ball differently and stretch out for new peaks, perhaps recovering the flamboyance of bygone days.

If you had asked any British international player who he would have chosen to replace Fouroux he would have gone for Astre, the elegant mover with the long pass, from Beziers. However, the French Selectors produced an inspirational choice which startled the rugby world.

Jerome Gallion of Toulon, an explosive runner and a brilliant passer, impressed a stunning maturity on the international scene. He toured Argentina with the French team at the end of the 1977 season which was his own first full season in the Toulon side. Such was his instant authority, he even captained France in one of their tour matches. He then captained France

Left:
The majestic Gallion kicks through against Scotland.

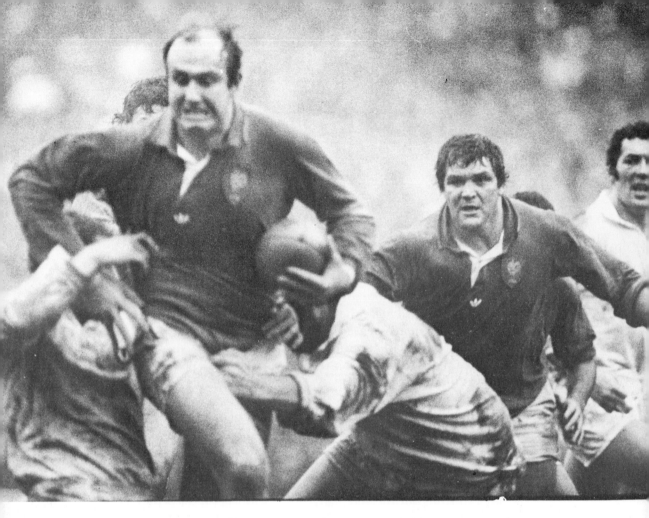

Under 23 against England. The French Selectors were so certain about the newcomer, they completley ignored the form of Astre. Was Gallion the new dimension they were seeking?

If Gallion's arrival was exciting, that of his chosen partner Bernard Vivies was mystifying. How could Romeu, the goal kicking specialist be ommitted? Tomeu, like Fouroux, was tactically sound. He knew all about kicking for control, but he could also run and pass with typical French delicacy too. More illogical still, Vivies played full-back for his club Agen. Only at Orrell, against the England Under-twenty threes had he turned to outside-half.

The changes in the centre and on the wing were much more understandable because this is where so much had disappointed in '77. Belascain ousted

Sangali and after a year of disqualification because of his club-hopping which is forbidden in France, Gourdon returned to join Averous on the wings. Thus reshaped France met England at Parc des Princes for the first match.

England surprised them for twenty minutes or so. Alan Old dropped a goal and the English pack, urged on by their new leader Bill Beaumont, made it known that they were happy to play a tough game. They made a target of the big lock Palmie.

Palmie had become a marked man because his name had recently come up in the French law courts. He was accused of committing what we would described as grievous bodily harm to a rugby opponent during a match. He had maimed the player whose sight had since been affected. That sort of action does

Bastiat — leading by example against Scotland.

not make you many friends, and Palmie quickly discovered that all England was happy to trample him into the ground if he fell over.

France got the expected win by 15 points to 6, but Vivies was nervous and unskillful. The back division only functioned with real menace when Aguirre rushed in from full-back. Gallion, however, was brilliant. Apart from him and Aguirre nothing had improved.

I have my favourtie memory of that match. Gallion received a ball from the line-out, thirty yards out, and sensing that the English pack were slavishly moving back and across behind their backs to cover, he darted right through the middle of them. It was a lightning, unorthodox touch; instinct — not planning, and dazzling acceleration to the try-line.

The experiment moved on to Murrayfield. In the rain France were down by 13-0. Surely the French Selectors were now paying the price for ommitting Romeu? Suddenly Aguirre confounded everyone by kicking a brilliant conversion from the touch line

Paparemborde steals away, whilst others are otherwise engaged.

Gallion displaying his
incredible speed from a
standing start.

Left:
Averous scoring against
England.

and three penalty goals which turned the
game France's way. The final touch was
provided by . . . yes, Gallion.

He kicked over a line-out, followed up
fast, much faster than poor Hegarty had
imagined possible, and he scooped up
the dropped ball to score. The road to the
second Grand Slam was widening, as
France left the field the winners by 19-
16. Only Wales were keeping pace, and
the Irish were hardly likely to do a giant-
kill in Paris.

How wrong we all were. Ireland and

France wanted the game postponed
because the pitch was like a skating rink,
all ice and rock hard. It was surprising
that someone did not get seriously
injured. France had replaced the lock
Imbernon with Haget up in Scotland and
Haget had done well enough to keep his
place for the rest of the season. Gourdon
had managed only a nervous and sadly
clumsy come-back and he forfeited his
place to Bilbao on the wing.

France scrambled home yet again by
the boot of Aguirre and the now regular

Haget towers over the obstructed Martin.

try of Gallion. The forwards pinned Ireland back for long periods but the tries never came. It was clear in the crowd that support was swelling for Romeu, and even Fouroux could be talked back to the captaincy perhaps. Poor Vivies looked every bit like a full-back playing at outside-half. He did some things tidily but he simply lacked the vision of an attacking player, or even a safe one, when confined to small spaces by fast breaking forwards.

I, for one, detected the frustrations affecting the play of Bastiat, the captain.

It was proof that winning the ball is not the end of the game. It is what you do with it that counts.

France defeated Ireland 10-9. Yes, it was that close. I ought to give due praise to the forwards. They are a hard rugby nation now, carefully tutored and cool when the going is tough. Long gone is that reputation for extravagance, of either brilliance or baffling incompetence. Back in the fifties the French could never fight back if they were down, but in the 70s the Latin temperament has been subjected to firm team-

Right:
Gallion breaks away from the Scottish pack.

48

Left:
Belascain in action
against Scotland.

Rives.

planning. The final match was against Wales and who was to say that they could not muster enough heart and skill to take a second Grand Slam in a row.

The history books show that Wales themselves won the Grand Slam and that match at Cardiff by 16-7. No one will forget what a wonderful sporting prospect it was. All Wales hoped that France would not recall Romeu to kick the goals in what was bound to be a tight match. On the wings Noves and Bustaffa replaced Bilbao and Averous.

Gareth Edwards and Phil Bennett that day surely taught the French Selectors all about control of play at half-back. Edwards, at the core of possession, forged such a game of anticipation and timing, he was able to sweep play forwards with long rolling kicks. Then when it mattered he could still dash away on his own, catching the French by surprise. The mere contrast of half-back play said it all. Gallion, at last, was subdued.

Thus French hopes foundered, but an analysis of that match proved other facts too. The Welsh shoved the French, and exposed the fallibility of the French scrummaging machine. In Paris, the year before, Wales had unwisely chosen light-weight men, Glyn Shaw and Derek Quinnell on the left hand side of the scrum, both fine players, but needing to be complimented by stronger team-mates at international level. France took the Grand Slam then. This time the Pontypool front row Faulkner, Windsor and Price, locked by Wheel especially, and Martin, did the trick. The brilliant back row of Rives, Bastiat and Skrela had less of a platform for attack this time.

Thus the search for French virtuosity in 1978 succeeded only in the per-formances of Aguirre and Gallion, though Belascain and Bertranne pro-duced some of the most shuddering tackling I have seen for a long time.

Will France next year realise their dream of virtuosity? Perhaps instead they will learn their lesson and recog-nise that true fifteen-man attacking rugby can only come with talent, and that talent can only find expression when based on control. If that has been digested then every home country may again find itself overrun by *tri-coleurs* in 1979.

Right:
Gourdon kicks out of defence.

Aguirre — full of concentration.

6 Wales go down under

GERALD DAVIES

No doubt when the Welsh players come to recollect their thoughts during future tranquility, they will remember the 1978 Tour of Australia in two distinctly separate ways — off the field and on the field. Off the field we were given a generously warm and hospitable welcome from the Australian people in general. The players in turn responded and reciprocated in like fashion to the reception; each one accepted his rôle as ambassador, shouldering his duties with ease and good humour. On the field it proved occasionally to be unhappy and frequently confusing so that by the end of the tour this gave rise to dour and downright unpleasant rugby. On balance it was a happy touring party but, in truth, it could not have gone on longer than its six week duration.

Arriving back in London on the 19th June a tired, dejected and sceptical team, it seemed a long time ago indeed since our eighteen hour flight from London Heathrow had ended with our arrival in Perth in Australia, Geoff "Fly me" Wheel was certainly glad to get his feet on firm soil again. We did get the impression by the end of the Tour that flying is not Geoff's favourite pastime. On the way out our one stop in Bombay did give him a few moments to gather his thoughts and wonder whether if they served Bombay Curry in Swansea, did they serve Swansea Curry in Bombay. We were not there long enough to find out the answer! In Perth, we celebrated the Manager's fortieth birthday;

Margaret, his wife, had sent cards and gifts with Derek Quinnell. J.P.R. was happy with his first rehearsal as Choirmaster, even with jet-lag. There was also the inspired pairing as room mates of Wheels and Grav: there couldn't have been a minute's silence in that room, what with the former's banjo playing and the latter's continuous singing of Welsh melodies. These activities never did manage to coincide. What the pairing did achieve, however, was that Grav's 'Windsor Davies' routine gave way to a successful imitation of Wheels. We were a happy band of men then.

The one discordant note was the weather. For those who had been on the 1977 New Zealand trip it seemed that the long wet winter was to continue. Perth had experienced a long dry spell but the weather had broken on our arrival and the rain bucketed down. Unlike New Zealand it was not to last long.

On Monday the training started or, as someone (Wheel again) was fond of saying, "Here we go for an hour and a half's savage entertainment". We had a full week before the first game and so we settled down diligently to prepare for the games ahead. Jet-lag is a very underestimated condition and it was nice to prepare the itinerary so that we had time to overcome its effects. It did mean, though, that the nine games were played in the four remaining weeks, so that once

Left:
Bastiat and Palmie feed Gallion against Scotland.

55

this week was over the games came thick and fast.

It was suggested that the first two games — against Western Australia and Victoria — would cause few problems. Rugby in these two areas was relatively weak, as the game is only of minor importance. Rugby league, Australian Rules and soccer form the staple sporting diet. This fact was borne out by the stadiums being half full even though the first game was played on Sunday afternoon and the second game against Victoria in Melbourne was played under floodlights. There were no other major attractions to compete with our matches.

Against Western Australia we duly won 32-3, all the points coming in a purple patch of 26 minutes in the first half when we had a strong wind advantage. Wales produced a more balanced display in Melbourne, when we won 52-3 at Olympic Park, site of the 1956 Olympics. Each game after this proved progressively to be harder either because of the quality of the opposition or the psychological factors involved.

As so often happens on tour we were forewarned — "Wait 'til you get to Sydney" — that events in New South Wales, where rugby is strong, might prove a lot more difficult. It turned out to be more difficult than anticipated. In my opinion we came up against the best team effort of the tour. Sydney were a talented team who were willing and able to play an all-round game of rugby football. They attacked us from the very beginning and from any position on the field. This was in no small part due to the positive leadership of Garrick Fay, at forward, and the superb distribution and inventiveness of Ken Wright at outside-half. In no time at all it seemed they had scored three good tries. It was an uphill struggle for us after that. But with application and perserverance we managed to take the lead with only a few

minutes remaining. Victory for Wales was denied, however, when Laurie Monaghan dropped a colossal goal from near the touch line on the 10 metre line to secure a win for Sydney. It was a feat he was to repeat in the final Test — from similar circumstances of a mis-kick to touch and a similar position on the field.

The next game against New South Wales Country at Cobar, because of our loss against Sydney, assumed an importance which it otherwise would not have had. This team was a representative side made up of players who did not live within the environs of Sydney. The players had to travel enormous distances to come to the game, and some of them argued afterwards that it was as much of an away game for them as it was for us. They hardly knew the town existed it seems. Be that as it may, we had a terrific welcome. Our arrival aroused curiosity and a great deal of interest. Twenty-six planes had been chartered from the outlying districts to fly supporters in for the game. But the weather took a turn for the worse and the rain and low cloud prevented twenty of them from coming in. Probably it was the only place on tour where the balance sheet did not show a profit and being the small union that they are, it was they who needed the money most. Under extremely wet conditions the team, and the pack in particular, played well and the game was duly won 34-0.

The next game against New South Wales was going to be hard because, apart from two recruits from the Countryside, it was the same team as at Sydney the previous Saturday. We did not want to lose to them again. In a difficult, uncompromising game where the Welsh forwards dominated, Wales ran out victors by 18-0. Apart from a superb, copy-book try, initiated by a Gareth Davies half-break, carried on by Ray Gravell and scored by Gareth Evans who feinted in and out, there was very little sparkling back-play.

Next stop was Queensland. They were recognised as the Champion State of Australia and were unbeaten at home for 3 seasons. In addition to this they laid claim, since they had beaten several New Zealand provinces, that they were the best team in the whole of the Antipodes. Canterbury had, however, jumped this claim the previous week and had won comfortably. In the event the Queensland game for Wales was to prove the most satisfying victory of the tour. It was also to be our last. The game proved, too, that Terry Holmes was coming of age and laid his own claim to a Test team place.

For the remainder of the week leading up to the first Test discussion of the pros and cons of the two Test teams and the eventual outcome of the Test took second place to the acrimonious discussion that centred around Australia's choice of referee. It's normal practice on tour for the Host Union to nominate a panel of referees from which the visitors take their choice. For some curious reason, this did not happen in Australia in 1978. Instead, according to the Tour's agreement, consultation was to take place on the selection of referees. No such consultation took place either. We were told who the referee was to be. To my mind no referee should be put in such an awkward and embarrassing position when there is so much disagreement. In act it proved embarrassing all round and a lot of goodwill was lost over the issue.

We lost the Test 18-8 and the Welsh players before, during, and after the game could not help feeling since the unilateral decision was stuck to so adamantly, that the dice was unfairly loaded against them.

This was the start of an unhappy week, because on Tuesday we went to Canberra and lost with the last kick of the match (21-20) to Australian Capitol Territory. The performance was described by Clive Rowlands as the worst display seen from a Welsh team. Wales, he reminded us, had not lost two consecutive games since 1963. It was not surprising therefore that feelings ran low indeed.

It was not to end there. During the course of the remaining week the full complement of the Test back-row of Derek Quinnell, Jeff Squire and Terry Cobner, our captain, were all doubtful for the Second Test. None of them recovered fitness in time. A newly constituted back-row of Stuart Lane, Clive Davies and J. P. R. Williams took the field. J.P.R., I feel, fulfilled a secret ambition by being selected to play at forward for Wales in a full International match. All three gave a tremendous amount of themselves. During the Test, too, we were to receive further set backs. Graham Price left the field after an ugly incident to be replaced by John Richardson who had shown consistently good form throughout the tour. Alun Donovan then left with wrenched ligaments to be replaced by Gareth Evans who himself soon suffered an injury — a depressed cheekbone which restricted his effectiveness. Both he and J. J. Williams (pulled thigh muscle) remained courageously on the field when in other circumstances they would have been replaced. The left hand side of the field was, therefore, hopelessly weak. With J.P.R. withdrawn from the forwards to play in his customary role of full-back, it left us exposed in the back-row. Fortunately none of these weaknesses was exploited at any stage during the game. It needed a dubious drop goal by Paul Maclean to win the game for Australia. For those with eyes to see, it clearly did not go between the uprights.

So in the middle of June Wales returned once more from an unsuccess-

ful tour to a major rugby playing country Are there any lessons to be learnt?

Whilst it is essential to have a week's respite after travelling to Australia before the first game, it is equally essential to maintain a balanced match programme. The match itinerary was as follows:—

Sunday	Western Australia
Wednesday	Victoria
Saturday	Sydney
Tuesday	New South Wales Country
Saturday	New South Wales
Tuesday	Queensland
Saturday	Australia 1st Test
Tuesday	Australian Capital Territory
Sunday	Australia 2nd Test

These games were compressed into four weeks. On occasions, as you can see, it did not leave time enough to recover from the previous game. This gave rise to a lot of injuries. It no longer makes sense even on a short tour, to take only 25 players. Twenty-one of these players are on call for every game.

In future it may be worth considering the wisdom of going on a tour such as this so soon after a major Lions tour.

Some of the players certainly began to feel weary of rugby towards the end.

The question of neutral referees is an old chestnut and all the more reason now to get rid of it once and for all. The list of confusing decisions and interpretations could fill this chapter, but to do so would sound too much like sour grapes. But would any of the Home Countries be happy, I wonder, to accept an invitation to play Wales at, say, Pontypool, Llanelli, Aberavon or at any other Welsh Club ground with 10 local players and the match to be refereed by a local man? This is meant in no way to reflect on the integrity of those people. I'm just wondering whether any of the Home Countries would like it, that's all. We were forced to accept a similar situation, without recourse, in Australia.

For me the wheel has come full circle. After the failure of Wales's tour to New Zealand in 1969, there followed an unprecedented period of Welsh rugby success. In 1978 the record books will show that Wales undertook an unsuccessful tour to Australia when they also lost two Tests. Will another Phoenix rise out of these ashes too?

Left:
J.P.R. operating in the pack.

7 Violence in Rugby

BARRY JOHN

'Thuggery' was very much on every one's lips after Graham Price's cheek bone was shattered by a blow from Steve Finane in the second test between Wales and Australia, and indeed this particular incident was only the high-light of a tour which had been played in a very unsatisfactory and unacceptable spirit. Clive Rowlands, the Welsh Tour Manager, came out strongly against such behaviour and the 'Price Affair' in particular, saying in his after-match speech in Sydney, "If this is rugby I want no part of it, and what an effect it must have had on the thousands of schoolchildren present." But weeks later, Australian coach, Darrell Haberlecht, attacked Rowlands for his remarks and plainly put the blame on the Welsh shoulders stating that Wales with their trampling in the rucks started it all off virtually from the commencement of their tour in Australia.

Naturally, one accepts that there will be conflicting points of view. In the past when similar issues have arisen, nothing being done, time took care of things. But this is more serious.

The unhappy incidents which marred the Australian Tour cannot lightly be dismissed, for whilst there are many who will say that rugby was always like this, it cannot be denied that virtually every tour nowadays involves an ugly incident or two: whether the tour be to this country or elsewhere.

The successful tour of the 1971 Lions to New Zealand was heralded every-where, but no account of that tour would be definitive if the game at Canterbury and the blatant use of thuggery to bring about victory was not fully chronicled. The '74 Lions Tour and it's mass punch-ups and '99' call; Keith Murdoch's sending home on the '72/3 All Blacks Tour and the bad feeling that existed between that party and nearly everyone; England's violent series against Australia in '75; the friction that existed between the '77 Lions and their hosts and press and latterly the Welsh Tour of Australia, allied to the fact that there are record dismissals from the field in nearly all grades of Rugby in this country, are all statistical proof that the game is becoming rougher and tougher.

Surely, even accepting the pressures of modern International Rugby and the demands of the various competitions, it cannot be allowed to degenerate towards levels where 'street corner' behaviour will become accepted as part of the game. David Hayward (who is a contributor to this book) told me "I was known as a hard player who relished the physical aspect of the game, but at no time did I deliberately go out to kick any other player or adopt a 'couldn't care less' attitude."

The game is hard enough as it is, and with players getting bigger, fitter and faster every year the accident rate is understandibly going to be greater. However, it is alarming to observe the sort of physical behaviour which is becoming the accepted norm, par-

Left:
Graham Price leaves the field with a broken jaw.

ticularly in the rucks. Several leading players have told me that when they fall on a loose ball they know that they will be kicked, raked or trampled, as though it was an unwritten clause in their contract. It infuriates me to see players racing in towards the ruck with no thought given to the whereabouts of the ball, and take off feet first with complete disregard to body and limb.

To me, it is an indictment of their personality, but amazingly, some seem proud of themselves and even more so, when they get a 'ticking-off' from the referee: as though it was an acknowledgement of some brave act. Well, what can be done about this serious state of affairs?

The onus, as far as I can see, is on the Clubs and particularly on the coaches. If the coaches are any good, not only will they imprint their style of play, but also their code of conduct on the Team.

The English Rugby Union has certainly not turned a blind eye to this serious problem, and have already made it known that any player who is over-physical in his approach and shows complete disregard to the spirit of the game will not be considered for representative selection. Such action could seriously undermine their chances at international level, but the R.F.U., to their credit, are prepared to put the game before success. This is a bold and very responsible approach to the game of Rugby Union Football and should be followed by others.

It would be stupid, naïve and unrealistic to assume that in a game such as Rugby with its physical side, everyone on the field would conduct themselves like perfect gentlemen and play like chessmen.

The players and referees alike accept that frustration and pure accident can trigger-off incidents where a fist or two will fly. The important factor is that these are not premeditated and are recognised as such, although a referee has every right to act and give marching orders in such cases. What concerns me is the cold, planned tactics, where it is quite obvious to everybody that there was no provocation whatsoever involved, as in the opening minutes of a game. Two of the most blatant illustrations of this 'hatchet' tactic was Canterbury's punching in the opening minutes against the '71 Lions; and the Australian forwards, who ran past the ball when they kicked off against England in Brisbane '75, and seemingly went in kicking and punching already designated English players.

However, it is the ruck which more often than not proves to be the catalyst, and sends players wild, as they see a team-mate unnecessarily hacked on the ground.

Whilst referees are prepared to act on punching, they are reluctant to act on the reckless approach of a player to a ruck — perhaps feeling that he is trying to be constructive.

Trampling and climbing in the rucks, in my opinion, is far more dangerous than throwing a punch, and although I have seen numerous players receive stern warnings as to their conduct, I have yet to see someone sent off for so-called trampling.

Referees should remember Kevin Kelleher's actions at Murrayfield in 1967 when he sent off the mighty Colin Meads.

Meads had already been warned and, although the incident (in which he flashed a boot at the ball which happened to be near David Chisholm's face) could be interpreted as 'going for the ball', Mr Kelleher was insistent that Meads had no real care whether he had kicked the ball or Chisholm, and so, he sent Meads to the dressing room — a courageous decision.

Our referees must be prepared to be courageous, and in return they must be supported by the relevant bodies, by punishing the offending players severely. Scotland showed the way two years ago and to their cost, when Gordon Brown was suspended for a lengthy period and missed the whole international championship. There has already been one court action (let us hope it is the last) indicating that the Rugby Authorities are prepared to act strongly and put their own house in order. But above all, it is the responsibility of those who select and prepare the teams, no matter what the level.

If they persist in selecting the undesirables, then, as far as I am concerned, they only condone such action and behaviour on the field — a very sad state of affairs indeed.

Bastiat and Bennett go for a quiet word.

8 A macabre year for the Scots

NORMAN MAIR

Last season Scotland played ten internationals all told at full international, B and Schools level — and lost the lot. It was the first time since 1968 that Scotland had lost all four of their championship matches and since the nadir of this calamitous campaign was reserved for the closing match, a 15-0 defeat against England, it seemed obvious not just that something had to be done, but that it had better be seen to be done.

The hope was that the Scottish Rugby Union would change the whole structure of their selection committee for, even within their own ranks, there were those who privately acknowledged that finding five good selectors from what is, for these purposes, only a fifteen-strong body, was a pretty tall order, to put it kindly.

After all, the six special representatives and the nine district representatives are apt often to owe their berths on the Union to qualities other than the ability to judge a player, blend a team, weigh an opposition — above all, it is liable to take a man so long to work his way on to the S.R.U. that, by the time he gets there, he is a little out of touch with the playing arena, though still, of course, capable of being an invaluable member of the Finance committee, a wow on the Entertainments . . .

What the more optimistic had envisaged — though no-one was saying it was all the selectors' fault, pretending there was talent to spare — was a selection committee with, say, two from the

Union, two from outside and the coach. What Scottish rugby got was far short of that but still a major concession — to wit, the elevation to the selection committee of the coach.

The first 'Adviser to the Captain' — as the S.R.U. defiantly dubbed him — for they had for long regarded the word 'coach' as about the dirtiest five-letter word in the English language, was, of course, Bill Dickinson. His appointment dated back to 1971, being made after the defeat from France but before that never-to-be-forgotten game with Wales which John Taylor won with what Joe McPartlin deemed the greatest conversion since St Paul's'.

Never again, swore the BBC's Alun Williams, would nineteen-eighteen connote for him the end of the Great War. After the match, the S.R.U. seemed almost as pleased in defeat as the Welsh were in victory and that night Dickinson was very much *persona grata* — but, though he lasted seven seasons, they apparently never trusted his judgement enough to make him a selector. A curious contradiction, you may think.

When Nairn MacEwan emerged as his successor last season, it was announced, somewhat cryptically, that he would be 'involved in selection', — which turned out to mean, would you believe, that he would be there all the way, until the selection committee actually got down to picking the team. Thus Scotland's coach remained in a position all too close to that of the foot-

Left:
Irvine — retired injured against France.

65

ball manager who has to carry the can if things go wrong but whose directors choose the team. That Nairn MacEwan fretted in this ambiguous rôle was common conjecture, but last season's dire results, paradoxically, probably helped his cause, presaging change. At any rate, when that splendid Scotland forward of yesteryear, Hamish Kemp, stepped down from the selection committee, it was to MacEwan that he gave way. All the other four selectors, though, remained — the argument apparently being that continuity was vitally important even if most outsiders might have concluded that, recent results being what they were, continuity was precisely what Scotland did not want.

Steeling oneself to take one last painful glance back over the past season, the Irish match will be chiefly remembered on two counts. First, there was the selectors' decision, much appreciated by the Irish coach, Noel Murphy, to field Andy Irvine on the right wing where, the way Scotland were shaping, he appeared extremely unlikely to see much of the ball. Nor did he, but then Scotland have a history of moving key players out of their optimum positions even when the player in question is the best man available for the berth — unlike, for instance, the Lions' Tour of South Africa in 1974 when J. P. R. Williams was the obvious first choice for full back and it was always

'Super Sub McKinney' — first touch and a match-winning try against Scotland.

Left:
Slemen breaks away from Morgan.

likely that Irvine would end up winning his Test place on the wing.

Arthur Dorward, The Gala, Cambridge University and Scotland scrum half, was once suddenly picked at stand-off for a national trial on the grounds that he had played there at his preparatory school. Doug Keller, the Wallaby flanker whom Scotland also capped, was no less mysteriously named at hooker in another Scotland trial while, strangest of all in the eyes of posterity, the season after Scotland won their last Triple Crown in the searing climax of 'Wilson Shaw's Match' at Twickenham in 1938, that particular hero found himself shunted to the threequarter line. The reward for which, in that 1939 season, was the antithesis of a Triple Crown, Scotland losing all three games.

But to return to the Irish match, there was, secondly, Douglas Morgan's decision, in the last ebbing throes of injury time, with the score 12-9 in Ireland's favour, to scorn an eminently kickable shot at goal in favour of a tap-penalty, going for a try, a win and a possible Triple Crown rather than what would have been, none the less, only Scotland's fifth away point out of a possible 34 in 17 matches on enemy soil. Scotland had not scored a try at

69

Lansdowne Road since 1970 and, at the fateful instant, for all their territorial pressure downwind in the second half, one was gloomily convinced that their next try at I.R.F.I. Headquarters was more likely to take another eight years than another 10 seconds. Had it come off, of course, to many Morgan would have been all kinds of a hero: as it was, he had to be philosophically content with oblique suggestions that he was bang in the running for Ireland's Sportsman of the Year award.

A fortnight after that agonisingly controversial defeat, Scotland were back at Murrayfield at bay to France, the Grand Slam champions of 1977. With Irvine restored to full-back and playing superbly and the new hooker, Colin Deans, showing up predictably well in the open, Scotland rapidly found themselves an electrifying 13 points to the good.

Barry John, earlier in the season, had reiterated his belief that one definite French weakness lay in dealing with the ball put through behind them on the floor. Significantly, Scotland's two tries — scored by, respectively, Dave Shedden and Andy Irvine — both came from searching, beautifully-struck, running downfield punts by Douglas Morgan, one with his left foot, one with his right.

Not so long ago, if France had found themselves thirteen points down in an alien land with the rain streaming down, the enemy could probably safely have relied upon Gallic temperament to do the rest. This modern France, having snatched 4 points back in the fleeting minutes before half-time, proceeded to exhibit what seemed to jaundiced Scottish eyes a positively Anglo-Saxon phlegm and patience. In the end, France won 19-16 and that though Morgan, without playing the ball first, had dropped a goal from what was in the jargon, an indirect rather than direct

penalty. The three points stood and, coming hard on top of the Ireland match, prompted Scotland's captain to remark, ruefully but cheerfully, "I am nothing if not controversial!"

Dropped back from wing threequarter to full-back in the French match after Irvine had had to retire injured, Bruce Hart had been some way short of his best but, two weeks later in Cardiff, with Irvine still out of action because of his damaged shoulder, he made sundry stirring contributions. In particular, he had two great tackles on Gerald Davies, the effect of which, as one remembers remarking at the time, was as startling as a tangible hit on a wraith. What is more, Hay had much to do with Jim Renwick's try, taking Ian McGeechan's pass on the burst before slipping the ball inside to Renwick who stepped back outside J. J. Williams with the kind of jink which had the Welsh acclaiming him almost as one of their own. In a better side, Renwick might well have emerged as the outstanding centre of the entire championship.

Hay's tackling was in rude and violent contrast to that of the Scotland pack which was execrable, the irony being that other considerations had led to the dropping of the best tackler in the pack, namely Sandy Carmichael. The grandson of Alex Bennett, who played football for Scotland and also for both Rangers and Celtic, A. B. Carmichael had, against Ireland the previous month, won his fiftieth cap. Came the closing weeks of the season and he announced his retirement, quietly revealing that he had for some time been struggling against a bad back.

Destined always to be coupled with Ian McLauchlan, Sandy Carmichael — who was awarded an M.B.E. for his services to rugby — will pass into legend as the first of his race to win 50 caps, but to me his name will always conjure up

Renwick slips out of Ward's tackle.

glorious tackling, hard, low and with that acceleration into impact which so often obliterates sidestep, swerve or change of pace. He was one of the cleanest of the great players but then, as one has observed before, when you tackle like the clap of doom you have no need to go round squaring up to people to prove your masculinity.

Wales won 22-14 with a try-score of 4-2 but, even allowing that most of

Scotland's most fluent football was played when the game was virtually lost beyond recall, things had at last begun to happen behind the Scotland forwards. Ian McGeechan, on his return to stand-off, had not been by any means flawless, but he played well enough to render relevant the words of the Welsh coach, John Dawes: "The *one* selection that worried us, the one we definitely did not want you to make, was the moving of Ian McGeechan up to stand-off. He's a good

little footballer, he's elusive and he's a good passer. To me, it is his best position."

Alas, McGeechan was injured between the Welsh match and the Calcutta Cup and, eventually, though he travelled to Edinburgh to work out with the Scotland team, was forced to pull out, his place going to Richard Breakey, a Fettesian like Ron Wilson, the stand-off against Ireland and France, but even taller, standing an elongated 6 feet 4 inches.

It is one of the curiosities of the sporting scene that Scotland have produced so many gifted little men in other realms of sport — men like Benny Lynch in boxing, Sandy Saddler in golf, Jimmy Johnstone in football — and yet so often in the post-war era have fielded stand-offs who looked almost like strays from the second row, albeit some were undeniably good footballers. Just as policemen used to have to be over 6 feet, so there are those in Scotland who suggested, not wholly facetiously, that some kind of reverse limitation should be applied in the matter of Scotland stand-offs.

In the event, Scotland were so badly thrashed in front by England that it would have taken the backs of the Golden Twenties, Nelson, Waddell and the Oxford three-quarter line, all their time to salvage much of a result. In a match which provided, by the standards of the modern era, one very quaint statistic in that Scotland did not have one kick at goal from inside the enemy half, Scotland sank to their first home defeat at the hands of the Old Enemy in ten years and, in so doing, failed to score a point against them on home soil for the first time since they were taken 18-0 at Inverleith in 1921.

Thanks to suspension and injury, Gordon Brown, the Lions' Test Lock, has not played for Scotland in the past two seasons and seven out of the eight inter-

nationals have been lost, the pack sadly lacking real body and core in his absence. He trained during the close season in the hope that his long lay-off, together with treatment, had done the trick with regard to that troublesome shoulder but time alone will tell what he has got left to give to Scotland.

Though Irvine was back for the England match, it was a bad season for injuries. That explosive ball-player David Leslie, was a grievous loss to a back row which was never really firing on all three cylinders.

Not that it did not all provide some black comedy. The selectors' decision to have two centres but no wing among their six subsitutes for the French match, duly tempted a humorous fate to decree that they needed, in the course of the match, to replace both wings but neither centre. There was, too, Graham Hogg's deliciously heartless quip to Dave Shedden after that infinitely plucky but lightly-built wing had been stretchered off yet again. "Next time," said Hogg, having come on as a replacement two matches in succession, "I'll just follow you down the tunnel."

Slice it where you will, as P.G. Wodehouse might have said, it was, despite an all-conquering early season tour of the Far East, a macabre year for the Scots — and ahead lay Argentina and the events of the World Cup.

In which connection — and remembering how the Welsh felt about the result against Scotland at Anfield and the manner of it — the crack of the season possibly belonged to Brian Fowler, the Ammanford club captain at a reception given to Lismore on the eve of the Wales-Scotland match in Cardiff. "We are sorry," he said, blandly, "to hear that Andy Irvine is out — but we are still expecting you to play a handling game, because we have heard that you have brought in Joe Jordan!"

9 Commentating – the next best thing!

NIGEL C. STARMER-SMITH

It's no simple transition from being a player to becoming a commentator — but, yes, you could say it's the next best thing! Principally, because you're there, be it Stradey Park, Ellis Park or Parc des Princes; so close to the game that it's as near as you can get to the action without being on the field itself. Yet there is a crucial difference. You are involved, but at the same time you must be detached; you're excited but you can't cheer; you follow every movement, but never give or take a pass; you are nervous, and perhaps like a player, exhausted at the end, but you haven't run a yard (sorry, metre!). You may disagree with a referee's decision, but you accept his final judgement — while at the same time appreciating, more than ever you did as a player, what a difficult, even impossible, task he has. And so it is on tour; you are with the team, but you are not, if you see what I mean.

Obviously, there are things you miss, for better or worse. Take training, for example (you can as far as I'm concerned and I think Gareth might agree!) especially those wet, windy nights, when three of the floodlight bulbs have blown, the bath water's cold, and Earl Kirton, or Bob Hiller are dissatisfied with your current efforts. I don't think anyone has quite understood the onus on the inside-half in training, and the one fact that has never been resolved. He has to be in two places at once; with the backs at all times passing the ball out, rehearsing the moves, as well as being in constant demand by the forwards, feeding the ball in — a source of endless criticism, or rather excuses, for hookers — or giving the calls and receiving the ball from line-out, maul or ruck.

I sometimes wonder whether the advent of squad training didn't owe something to the fact that coaches could never resolve the problems created by splitting a team into two, and finding that both units are incomplete without their own scrum-half. By the way, does anyone else stop to consider the enormous repertoire of calls and signals that a scrum-half has to assimilate? There are the back division signals— **full-back in, blind-side wing in, crash ball, Rangi, miss one, two, dummy, scissors,** and so on; then the back-row moves, with flankers and Number Eight in varying combinations, short penalty moves; all the line-out signals (which the scrum-half usually gives), names, numbers, foot or hand signals, which ever are used by your club side; and there are individual relationship calls with different fly-halves and hookers. And who has to know each and every one? — that's right, Number Nine! By about November you've just about absorbed the repertoire of your club side, alone enough to tax a talented tic-tac man! But then what happens? You play for another side — a county team, or something else, and what's the result? A completely different set of signals. The line-out call "6-19-4" becomes "Cauliflower" or "Caerphilly". The threequarter move

"All Black" becomes "Springbok", and vice-versa. And so it goes on, with regional and trial sides, maybe even international teams; everyone just assuming the scrum-half has a computer brain.

No, this isn't meant to be an apologia for witless scrum-halves, simply an observation. Oh! And while I'm on the subject, isn't it odd how the inside-half is so often at the *extremis* in criticism. If his side wins, the scrum-half was brilliant, as a matter of course, but if the team loses who's the fall guy — the same player. And both assessments are so often as not wildly wrong. It's about as absurd as the way wingers get lauded to the heights for catching a ball and falling over the line for a try. You know the sort of thing in the headlines:

"Two-try Jenkins inspires Fyffes Bananas to thrilling last-minute victory over British Rail Maintenance."

The fact that Jenkins had earlier waved his opposite number through for two soft tries, and dropped three other scoring passes, is usually totally ignored. But Jenkins with his little white ankle socks, clean knees, and tight short shorts is the hero, at least as far as he is concerned. I digress. The point I was originally trying to make was that I do miss those midweek evening or Sunday morning sessions — like a bad cold!

Sitting in the commentary box there are a lot of things that happen on the field that can't be seen, or heard. For example, there are only hints of the intimacies of that exclusive private war, the front-row battle, that can be observed from the stands. I don't mean the rare vicious outbreak that the media love to highlight, the eye-gouge, kick or punch. (Why do punches on the field so often miss their target, by the way?). No, it's the Mickey Burton back-chat, the Windsor wise-crack, the knowing glare, the shuddering impact. There's the sort

of moment when, for instance, at half-time in a game at the Arms Park against Cardiff, the Oxford skipper, Tommy Bedford, harangues the Varsity team with a verbal onslaught in a very Springbok accent which is principally directed at a displeasing scrum-half: "Nawgel, ew minny tarms eff I ad to tell yew, fer Crysek min break — B-R-A-K-E!" Collapse of stout team talk to gales of educated laughter from the other thirteen. Or Bob Hiller, freely dispensing advice to the man with the whistle, taken to task, and to one side by a referee on the verge of losing control, in a game between Surrey and somebody:

"Hiller, I'm fed up with your non-stop banter; who do you think's refereeing this game, you or me?"

"Neither of us."

The spectator, or commentator, misses out, too, on the changing-room scenes. Nervous jokes, which are met with nervous laughter; peg-hanging rituals or Bucknall's stud-less boots. The Quins game at Twickenham when, ten minutes to kick-off, Bristol were frantically warming-up in that old-fashioned ritual of mass, on-the-spot sprinting to 10 — a sound deemed to intimidate the occupants of the neighbouring changing-room. Our skipper, Hiller (again!) anxious to preserve his efforts for the game only, and not wishing to be 'out-psyched' by the opposition, observed that we'd better do something. He called upon his half-changed motley crew (three of whom had yet to arrive) to counter with a pounding of the hands on the benches to make a comparable 'warlike' noise! It makes one wonder whether the Quins might have done better to introduce a pre-match 'Haka' to their game — at least we usually had all 15 present by the time we went on the field! Again, there was the day of the Long Buckby Sevens Tournament, when I was playing for Gosford All Blacks against

Stewart and Lloyds in the semi-final and the referee stopped the game because his toupée had fallen off. I wonder if that's covered in the laws?

So many incidents one can recall, just as you miss the bias of club, or national, pride in your team when Harlequins or England take the field. It's frightening how easily one can detach oneself from what you might think is an unquenchable prejudice when you are in an impartial commentating role. I suppose, if anything, one's caution may tend to make one slightly slanted in favour of the other side.

But in translating from the rôle of player to spectator, one thing you don't forget: how the spectator's different perspective on the game so often makes him ignorant of the truth of the matter. Opportunities, opposing strengths and weaknesses look so much more obvious from the stand, and so they are bound to do. No doubt they would to the players, too, if they had the advantage of seeing the game unhindered from above, remote from the physical involvement. It's the 'clever Dicks' in the stand who've either forgotten what it was like to play, or never did, who can repeatedly annoy with their 'after the event' obvious observations. The game you see from a distance is not identical to the one on the pitch — little things that can't be seen, or heard, from afar can make all the difference to a player's action — the awkward bounce, or angle, of a ball, the obscured vision, the mis-heard call, the un-noticed slight injury, the captain or pack-leader's deliberate instructions, and more besides. What does the spectator know of these?

Nothing can replace the sheer exhilaration, the challenge, the thrills or disappointments, and the fun of taking part, but at least commentating has more than its fair share of compensations because you are *there*. The experiences are

unending and contrasting: the euphoria of being present in Port Elizabeth at Willie-John's greatest moment of triumph in 1974, in Boet Erasmus Stadium, and at the joyous celebrations that followed; the bitterness of Ellis Park and the All Blacks - Springboks confrontation of 1976; the achievements and frustrations of the Lions in 1977, from the top international matches right down the scale. Treasured individual moments, too, like Bennett's try for the Barbarians in the Mobbs Memorial Match two years ago; Cobner's performance of character against Canterbury on the last Lions tour; 'Nipper' Rees, who once won the Army Cup Final, for the Royal Regiment of Wales, as near single-handed as can be in a fifteen-a-side game; Duckham in his hey-day; Catchpole behind a beaten Wallaby pack; or Gibson, most of the time.

In trying to convey the feelings of the moment to the viewer or listener, commentating does have its hazards. How much, or preferably little, information does a viewer require? What depth of knowledge of the game of rugby can one assume the majority of the audience to possess? and so on. Of the more obvious and immediate hazards rugby seems to suffer less than many other sports — notably the classic 'gaffes'. A boxing commentary, for instance, that included the line 'I'm sure Chris Finnegan would give his right arm to be a southpaw', or in rowing 'And it's either Oxford or Cambridge'; in cycling, 'And there you see the Russian, just out of sight', in cricket, 'And there's Colin Cowdrey, crouched in the slips, legs apart, waiting for a tickle', and so many more. In rugby no comparable quote comes to mind, though I do recall a slight confusion surrounding the description of a kick to touch by a recent Swansea and Scottish International winger, and the remark on a 'close-up' that followed: 'That was Lewis's Dick!' Not that rugby commentary doesn't have its problems, like the wearing of 'wrong' numbers, or, worse still, letters, by the players — unannounced changes by the touring Japanese, Tongans or Fijians can be especially confusing — or the interpretation of refereeing decisions which can bemuse spectator and player alike.

But while there's so much good sport and good rugby company to enjoy around the world, there's one more serious note on which to end this frivolous writing which concerns an increasing worry that I have for the future of the game. It doesn't need Wales's recent experiences in Australia, the Lions in New Zealand, court cases or other incidents of which we are all aware, to bring home the effect on rugby football, and its popularity as a players' game, of violent play on the field. Few outbreaks of viciousness there may be, too many there certainly are. It is time all concerned took stock of the situation; the game is getting too serious. Sometimes it is hard to believe that players are taking part for enjoyment, and not for money. Or are the *reasons* for playing rugby football changing as well!

10 The immortal dive of P.C. Mog

RICHARD BURTON

Once upon a time when I was a child, somewhere around the neolithic age, and the game of Rugby, West of the Severn tunnel, was played savagely for the most part by six-days-a-week and reluctant pelunkers, there were two rugby players. One was a man called Morgan (Mog) Hopkins. The other was a certain Arthur Bassett. Both, I think, were policemen. There is no way of verifying these facts in Budapest, and the Danube which is flowing past me as I write, like Ole' Man River, don't say nuthin'. In any case it doesn't matter for they both played for my local team. This particular team was called Aberavon. Hopkins was a centre-threequarter and Bassett was his wing.

Mog Hopkins handled the ball and passed it with all the delicacy of a man throwing a suspect hand-grenade. It was precisely delivered, with almost no touch, to the dynamic Bassett and written on it in impeccable Welsh were the words "Not too dangerous but handle with care, it won't blow up but the referee might." For his passes were so timed that with Bassett's tremendous lust for the ball the foolish referee might think it was not lateral but forward. I cannot think of a more perfect passer of the ball at that time. I have seen great ones since.

Incidentally, to give you an idea of Mog Hopkins's character, he was the policeman who having charged a man for some slight felony, was the first to leap across the court-room and congratulate him when the case was dis-missed. It happened in Gorseinon, I seem to remember. There was much astonished embarrassment.

There was no question that Bassett was a great wing-threequarter. Given the ball with half a pace to move in, he seized upon the idea of the corner-flag as if his ultimate hunger on the face of this sad earth was to eat the wood and the flag, and indeed anybody who came between. He and Hopkins and the corner-flag made mad music together. There was no argument that Bassett was infinitely 'cappable' but we were, in those days, an unfashionable team, and in order for Bassett to get a cap and be noticed it was necessary for him to move to a more glamorous side and the most glamorous was, and still is, I suppose, Cardiff. Even the present London-Welsh and the harsh Coventry and the farmers of Northampton and the cold theoriticians of Newport do not quite match the sometimes subdued but mostly blatant brilliance of Cardiff. So Bassett moved to Cardiff and inevitably got his 'caps'. We all felt betrayed but Bassett was ambitious; and it's no use trying to play Hamlet with an audience consisting of two men and a dog. Later and lamentably, Bassett went 'North'. Lamentably for us I mean. For Wales I mean. We have lost so many great players to the 'North'. If we could only have kept them economically we would have remained unbeaten for half a century. Risman and Randell Lewis and Ossie Griffiths and Sullivan and who

79

knows how many went cloth-capped to the 'North'.

But back to the story as I remember it. Bassett was in his prime and playing for Cardiff and Wales and he came home to play for Cardiff against Aberavon. By this time Mog Hopkins had retired into second-class rugby.

Now at this time we had a full-back of exquisite culture. His name was Tommy Owen James who moved balletically like a Nureyev into the proper position at the right moment and right or left-footed curled the ball caressingly into the right or left and perfect edge of 'touch'. Tommy Owen James accidentally played for Wales. I say 'accidentally' because he was kept out of the Welsh team by more obviously ostentatious players, and no offence to anybody including Vivian Jenkins, for Jenkins was about as good as one could get.

The match took place on the Monday of the Easter week-end — but it was badly marred or we thought it was marred — by the spraining or the breaking of Tommy Owen James's ankle two days before against Neath or Maesteg or Bridgend or whichever back-smashing local derby it happened to be. And here we were, against the immortals of Cardiff, without a full-back. What was there to do? Where to search? Who to find? I mean, for the sake of verisimilitude, this was Cardiff who had internationals — and still do I expect — in their 'B' team, and they already had a double legend in Wilfred Wooller and Cliff Jones. Because of a certain eminence borrowed from a brother who had played top-stuff rugby for some years I was permitted in to see the two abject dressing rooms and was allowed to watch the players as they muttered and moaned and embrocated themselves. To my delight at the time, but my regret now, Cliff Jones was unable to play, but I saw Wooller as plain as somebody once saw Shelley.

There was nothing to do but ask Mog Hopkins to come back. He was such a superbly co-ordinated player that he could play in any position except possibly 'hooker' as I think he refused to be supported. But there he was, back at full-back.

I saw Bassett too. He must have been about five feet ten or eleven inches, but in those days of the Welsh Wars when Neath cancelled all matches with Aberavon *sine die;* and the Barbarians cancelled all matches with Neath forever; when to go to play against Pontypool was to invite a certain mutilation and possible death; when indeed so many matches were abandoned because of their ferocity that there was a time when we seemed to have no fixtures at all against anybody except the juvenile London Hospitals, because obviously if somebody fractured a skull there was no need to ask for a doctor, for there were at least fifteen on the field. Or maybe fourteen depending on which side had fractured the other's skull. As I was trying to say Bassett could not have stood more than about six feet at most, but to my dwarfed eyes he stood at least six feet five. And as for Wooller . . . Ah well, we stood no chance. What were we going to do with him? A man who could punt the ball a million yards into the unreachable far corners of the field as if it were an afterthought. A man, who in full stride, didn't bother to swerve around lesser people but ran right over them like an aristocratic train. And outside him, you must remember, was Bassett.

I went into the Aberavon dressing-room. Mog Hopkins was chatting and completely relaxed as if he had just been called in to play, rather condescendingly, for Tonmawr against Pontrhyd-yfen. Walter Vickery was picking up people because he didn't have his weights with him and — for a time — used me as an Indian club. But, baby as I was, I was aware of the tension — Wooller and Horace Edwards and Bassett in the next room!

And so to the match. To a dispassionate watcher it must have worn on like an old shoe. Aberavon, being the under-dogs, pressed like demented launderers. Cardiff, despite their superiority, were driven into mediocrity by the murderous hammering of our back-row and indeed anybody who could stop that ball from going out to the backs — especially Wooller and Bassett. But it was bound to happen. And it did.

Thre was a scrum on the Cardiff five-yard line. It was Cardiff's loose head. I was standing with my brother-in-law and his father. Cardiff won the ball. The Cardiff inside-half took it like a bad idea from a bad God. He deliberately missed his outside-half and the ball went back to Wooller like a scream.

"O'r Arglwydd," I muttered in my brain. "Don't worry," said my brother-in-law Elfed, "it's a Cardiff trick, Wilf is only going to clear for a long touch." "Paid a becso," said Elfed's father, "dim ond 'long punt' yw e'." ("don't worry — it's only a long punt.").

But Wooller twisted and burst and slung the longest pass I had ever seen, one-handed, across the field to Arthur Bassett. He had roughly 90 yards to go and Wooller, with one magnificent turn and break had made him clear of the field. And Bassett went. There was indeed nothing between him and the try-line except Mog Hopkins.

Except that Mog, having watched the match rather idly from a distance, for Aberavon had pursued Cardiff with such relentlessness that he had hardly been called upon to touch the ball or put foot to it all afternoon, wasn't there. He was having an amiable chat with somebody in the crowd. With the great moan from the throng and all the instinct that is part of a great player, he realised that he was dressed up for something other than arranging to go to the Grand Hotel for sausages and mash after the match.

He started to move like slowly gathering lumber. Bassett was going like venom out of a cobra and knowing perhaps that his old friend Mog had slowed down, he made the error of swerving in towards him, in order for him to swerve outside him with his superb acceleration, perhaps out of a feeling of superiority — though I'd like to think not, but Mog Hopkins with the expertise of a milk train knew that if he could get to the points before they changed, he could stop the Express.

It was for me a few seconds ripped out of eternity.

One had the impression of T.N.T. moving in one direction and slow-burning gun-powder in the other. It was a parabola of exquisite mathematics. Would the two curves meet? My stomach turned into warm water. Would the thickening milk-train catch the lean express? Pure mathematics could never have stopped Bassett, but pure mathematics is a kind of poetry, and like poetry depends on the human personality. And involved here were human personalities.

Einstein proved that the shortest distance between two points is a curve. Bassett believed him. Hopkins was old-fashioned and believed with Euclid and Pythagoras that the shortest distance between him and Bassett was a straight line.

The straight line destroyed the curve. Just in front of the old grand-stand Mog caught the great Bassett. Only barely. I mean very barely. Only by one ankle. But he caught him.

It was a moment of great triumph. My stomach turned back into muscle and intestines and the warm water had turned cold.

My mind may play me tricks and I am sure that Mr. Bassett and Mr. Hopkins and Mr. Wooller will accuse me of distorted memory, but I prefer my memory of the truth to the truth itself.

Because of that moment I have virtually forgotten everything else about the match.

Who won?

11 Wales's Triple Triple

BARRY JOHN

Wales's defeat in the Tests against Australia in the summer was a blow, but it cannot cloud the fact that Phil Bennett and his historic Welsh team proved yet again that it takes qualities above skill and technique to achieve success at International level. The exception, of course, being the game against Scotland. There, moments when only tremendous belief in themselves and courage, got them through: the same unyielding courage they applied in the crucial stages against England, Ireland, and France — but success here was due to a total commitment by the pack allied to several superb individual performances behind the scrum.

In terms of individuality it is virtually impossible to state beforehand who is likely to be Wales's prominent figure, simply because there are so many capable of 'turning it on' that day. However, what can be guaranteed is that the Welsh performance very rarely drops below a certain standard. Their level of consistency is incredibly high, they make few mistakes and even under pressure demonstrate amazing composure.

Every team is capable of an exceptional performance, but the truly great teams must possess a high basic game and the ability to adapt and change according to play and conditions — this is Wales's great *forte*.

Bennett's team is ideally equipped with the right combination of experience and expertise. There are moments in their play when you might

think they are scarcely in top gear, but the trick — the deception — is that these boys create time for each other combined with confidence and that's the way to win.

Rugby is, of course, about winning — but such is the stature of the Welsh team at present that the *quality* of winning particularly at Cardiff is equally important. Perhaps the public, as well as the players themselves, are asking too much — but then it is this strange self-limiting trait which in the end, I believe, is Wales's strength.

Welsh Rugby of the last three years has been distinctively different from that of previous years. It may have settled into a predictability and not be as pleasing to the eye as the French game or games of the early seventies, but there is no denying its effectiveness. Look at the record book. The present Welsh pack is the strongest Wales has fielded for many years and so, this inevitably will influence the tactical approach by the team. Bennett and his backs are mainly second-phase attackers, using the set play to create pressure positions. Rarely do they attack from set-play and although the use of Ray Gravell and Steve Fenwick to crash through the middle to set up the mauls and rucks in mid-field paid undeniable dividends, there were many occasions when some swift passing and the stretching of the opposition defence would surely have proved far more fruitful.

Steve Fenwick is really something of

Bennett in action against France.

an enigma as far as centre play is concerned, and it must be accepted that orthodox mid-field play will be difficult while Fenwick is around. He cannot be compared with any other centre and it seems that he has found his own 'coaching manual for centres'!

There is nothing classical about his play and his basic premise is that he must attack the ball at all times. He really has an uncanny ability of being in the right place at the right time and whatever the situation, he is ideally equipped to act. He is able to kick well with both feet and

Bennett in action against France.

strong enough to knock over the most determined opponent or to lead his own counter charge. Fenwick's wonderful *vision* was in evidence when flicking a 'blind' overhead pass to J. J. Williams over in Dublin for that crucial try. Perhaps more importantly he is endowed with an ability to harvest points. Fenwick's easy-going nature and marvellous temperament allows him to take everything in his stride and several of his long-range penalties proved to be decisive. For a player who does not 'look' a centre Fenwick has many 'plusses' to

Bennett waits for Gravell's pass, but is already looking for gaps.

Jim Renwick tackles J. J. Williams, and the ball goes forward.

his game. He is undeniably individual, a 'one-off' and along with the powerful Ray Gravell he forms a formidable half of an ideal pair: able to play this physical game that Wales have opted for in recent years.

There has been of late far too much of this physical play when some marvellous opportunities to run and beat the opposition by speed of foot and hand have been squandered in place of muscle power.

With Wales's National Grand Slam team providing this year the shop window for the game it is inevitable, I suppose, that many other teams emulate their tactics. It is indeed difficult to find new up-and-coming centres blessed with a sharp eye for an opening and possessing the strength and speed to go through the gap. Far too many players in all positions are programmed to taking a member of the opposition out of the game. This slows the momentum of the attack in instances where there were many more attractive alternatives available.

Rarely does one see a perfectly delayed and timed pass putting a team-mate into the gap. Cardiff's Gareth Davies is such a player and no wonder the Cardiff backline prospered last season with the powerful Pat Daniels reaping marvellous rewards and fellow centre Mike Murphy, perhaps a little underestimated, another who can create time and deliver telling and decisive passes.

Even the great Gerald Davies benefitted, for there is no doubt his greatest moments last season were in the blue and black jersey and not in the red jersey of Wales with his 4-try game against Pontypool in the Welsh Cup the highlight. Aberavon's Neil Hutchings was the only centre I saw last season take a swing in at his opposite number, commit the tackle and then move majestically away again. There is a difference in taking a player 'on' and taking a player 'out'.

The loss of possession in a tackle is not a knock-on under the new laws, and the ever alert Steve Fenwick follows up . . .

Players must realise that if they take an oppoenent 'on' one of two things can happen — he can beat his opposite number or be stopped, and if they are well coached they will know what to do in either case. Gravell is most certainly not all muscle. He possesses a fine rugby nature and an awareness of players in better positions. At the present time his play seems to be plainly dictated by the passes he receives. Gravell can read situations, being able to 'chip' delicately and deliver well-timed passes. Unfortunately he does not seem to have had many real opportunities to show his creative skill and basic rugby ability. These were, after all, the qualities which brought him into the Welsh team in the first place.

With Bennett and his centres geared to taking the play down the centre of the field Gerald Davies and J. J. Williams are not employed as fully as one would like but such is the greatness of these two superb (gifted though different) wings, that they still contribute greatly: and when the isolated chance arrives to finish off a movement, they have not forgotten the way to the line, as J.J. showed in Ireland. Davies and Williams are excellent all-round footballers — nowadays a wing requirement. It is no longer enough just to have a blistering burst of speed — like Mike Sleman and Peter Squires (England). Williams was a Welsh Secondary Schools fly-half whilst Davies gained his first 14 Welsh caps at centre and played much of his junior

Right:
Gravell breaks through the Scotland defence and . . .

. . . to pick up and score.

rugby at fly-half, so both are fully conversant with working in tight corners and linking with supporting players. The perfect illustration was J.J.'s inside pass to Bennett under extreme pressure which resulted in Wales's second try against France. J.J. could so easily have been run out of play.

Whilst accepting that the Welsh pack had a marvellous season, it was a tragedy

that so little was seen of Gerald Davies and J. J. Williams. To attack down the flanks and use their natural skills and talents would have added another exciting new dimension to the team and it was sad, particularly against Scotland, to see Davies holding his head in his hands with frustration as superb possession was kicked away for position when he was perfectly positioned with

. . . scores his first try for Wales.

Right:
Bennett chips through to pressurise the Scottish defence.

yards in which to work. There was a dearth of new ideas, certainly. What we saw at this time was pressure, discipline, control and moments of pure magic: those peculiar talents of Edwards and Bennett along with Fenwick's 'one man show' in Dublin which ultimately toppled the rest.

Maybe I am looking for too much from this team; it is simply that I feel that they are not doing full justice to their own collective ability. They have provided some moments which sent the blood racing but they have noticeably become the rare moments of Welsh rugby play.

Gareth Edwards was my player of the year. Considering the standards he has set himself this is in itself an achievement — for only when you appreciate how fantastically high these standards are can you make a faithful judgement. There were crucial moments in virtually every game where his own judgement and subsequent action was supreme. At Twickenham it was his amazing kicking, where even the slimy, heavy conditions could not affect his slide-rule accuracy.

He kept the pressure on England in the second-half knowing full well that it was pointless being too ambitious in such conditions and that to preserve and keep the ball in front of his forwards and

Cobner wants more from his pack.

Quinnell breaks from a scrum, with Edwards available.

thereby turn the England defence would eventually bring about the chances which Phil Bennett dutifully converted into match-winning points. This was a perfect instance of experience being used to the full: knowledge of the requirements of the day; and going no further.

Scotland was a disappointing game all round — even allowing for the bitterly cold weather — and although Edwards was guilty of not releasing the ball on a couple of occasions in the last quarter it served to remind him, I feel, that even *he* is not above criticism.

If that was the case, it worked wonders — for in Dublin he rifled out the most amazing sequence of passes in any one of his 53 internationals, and under extreme and robust pressure — particularly in the lines-out when Moss Keane and company marched through so easily onto him. There were numerous occasions when he was bowled over as he released the ball but at no time did he take his eye off Bennett. Probably unnoticed by many, this singular factor enabled Wales and Bennett to dampen the Irish spirit. It was a day which so nearly brought the Irish back from the dead.

Should Edwards have retired at the end of last season, then he could not have wished for a more combative game to end with than that against the French — particularly against Jerome Gallion, heir pretender to his European throne. Whilst France and Gallion started with

pace and purpose and swept into a 7-0 lead, it was five minutes of vintage Edwards which brought Wales back into the game.

A couple of seering diagonal kicks gained position, picked up the momentum of the game and were followed by a towering drop-goal for much-needed points. It was these that made both the players and spectators believe in themselves again. Almost immediately another pressure position was gained with a torpedo-like sixty-yard touch-finder on the right, and Wales did not leave until Bennett had scored his first try. There are moments in sport when it needs an exceptional player, both in per-

Right:
Bennett scores against France: a collector's item of fly-half tries.

'You're the culprit,' says Quinnell.

sonality and skill, to raise his team from near despondency. Edwards did this midway through the first-half and had he not, France and not Wales would have won the Grand Slam.

After that, the Welsh pack gained parity, while a frustrated Bastiat became somewhat physical. He did not enjoy the same treatment when Quinnell stood up to him! Belatedly the giant French captain collapsed after the Quinnell skirmish. It was hardly an 'incident'. Quinnell was afterwards heard to remark, "If *I* had gone down like that — my father would have disowned me."

It does show the value of an Edwards in a team for his presence alone has a definite and distinctive effect on the opposition as well as team-mates.

This also applies to his partner, Phil Bennett. It would be unjust to look at the achievements of the Welsh team and not recognise fully the value of the contribution made by Bennett and Edwards. It would also be unfair on Brynmor Williams, Terry Holmes, David Richards and Gareth Davies, who toured Australia, to suggest that Wales would have won in Australia had Bennett and Edwards gone, for conditions of play and other factors make it vastly different to playing in this country. Obviously, to lose such an experienced pair is a severe blow, but the events of the tour suggest that it is highly unlikely that even the world's number one pair would have been able to make a contribution. As it turned out, two of the great successes of

Right:
J.P.R. attempts to break a tackle.

Gravell applauds his captain's first try against France.

the tour were Terry Holmes and Gareth Davies.

Bennett had an excellent season after the traumas of New Zealand with the '77 Lions, displaying wonderful composure and kicking easily with enormous effect in all games. His two fine tries against France came just when they were needed — yet another indication of a player turning up trumps at the right time. Wales are well endowed with such players.

Bennett's second try was a collector's item as far as fly-halves are concerned. He showed great courage in getting into the area where anything could happen as desperate defenders attempted to save a score. There was also one delightful moment from the Welsh captain when he just beat Sklera to a loose ball and when it seemed that the French flank forward would engulf him, Bennett, to everyone's surprise, flicked the ball between his legs straight to Steve Fen-

Pontypool concern!

Wheel takes on the French.

wick's hands, who counter-attacked on the left. Again a demonstration of that extra quality in Bennett's game. Of course, one cannot think of Bennett without thinking of his goal kicking, which has won so many games for Wales. As John Reason rightly says, 'it is suicidal to take the field now without a recognised goal kicker or two and the fact that Wales have been so superior in this department (largely through Bennett) has made the difference between Triple Crowns and Grand Slams in recent years'. Although all the Welsh backs had individual moments during the season, rarely did they produce a sustained period of combined play and this undoubtedly was responsible for J. P. R. Williams being more of an

orthodox full-back than in previous years.

There are definite signs that J.P.R. is not as quick or sharp as he has been but his defence was again outstanding, particularly in the French game. J.P.R. has still much to offer in attack — but others will have to assist him more, where the faster transference of the ball is an absolute essential. I also feel that he is best supporting the wings on the inside where his strength can break the covering tackles going in the opposite direction — but first the ball must reach the wings.

The Welsh forwards, without completely annihilating any pack, provided a fine platform on which Edwards and Bennett were to build and dictate. The famed Pontypool front-row never flinched and they stuck stubbornly to their task against the massive French trio. Frankly, set scrums are becoming something of an ugly excercise these days and often dangerous. There are far too many collapsed scrums which are not only illegal but could easily lead to serious neck and back injuries — as has been the case in junior rugby. Although referees are far quicker to act these days it is desperately difficult to sort out who is doing what to whom in the scrums. It's as though there's a bluff, double bluff and

so on to fool the referee. The standard trial of strength between the front-rows is an accepted and necessary practice but this should not persist throughout the game, it really is becoming time-consuming and an eye-sore.

The Welsh pack was a cohesive unit and their ball winners showed discipline in releasing the ball to Edwards. As ever Alan Martin was a valuable ball winner in the middle of the line-out, at his best in the second-half against England. He and Geoff Wheel complemented each other perfectly. Wheel displayed some

Right:
Nelmes, Cardiff's new Captain and English prop.

Quinnell hands off Biggar.

. . . now for McHarg.

Left:
Gareth's last game for Wales.

zest for open play and he was conspicuous in several combined forward handling movements during the campaign. His real value was in the mauls where his immense strength was responsible for gaining the most valuable possession of all. Cobner, Quinnell and Squire pressurised relentlessly and are ideally equipped for close support work. Although there were claims that their mobility was suspect, at no time was this really evident. Defence is very much a part of the back row play and all three produced many decisive tackles

particularly inside their own 22 metre line, while a couple of cross field covering tackles by Cobner against Scotland were of the Alun Pask variety.

This team has already proved itself but how long has it to go? How strong are the reserves in certain key positions? A lot could and is likely to happen in the next twelve months. With Gareth Edwards retirement the implications are far more than merely filling the No. 9 jersey. As Phil Bennett is likely to play for another two or three years, how will a

. . . the line in sight . . .

new scrum-half affect him and the play of his mid-field?

Terry Holmes has now overtaken Brynmor Williams as Edwards's understudy, and Gareth Davies is now a genuine threat to Bennett's position after his mature play in both Tests against Australia. The traditional qualities in a Welsh fly-half were those of being tricky, elusive and able to beat a man on a sixpence even under extreme pressure — in a nutshell, he was *instinctive.* Now, many of those situations have been eliminated as the legislators have created more room for him to operate — in fact, a little too much room — for it gives him time to think!

Obviously, fly-halves must still have

the ability to beat a man with either a side-step or a swerve, but whereas before they were high on the list of qualities, they have now been overtaken by feint, insinuation, and a calculating, disciplined and shrewd mind. The art of kicking has become even more important. A fly-half must be able to kill time and create a situation whereby his backs are given the ball as their predecessors were many years ago, and where their instinctive ability could again be given a chance to flower. Gareth Davies is such a player. Always threatening himself, he is completely aware of the situation and the positions of those around him. In fact, there is little to worry about at half-back; it's at three-quarter that Wales are short of quality

104

cover; although, looking at the other home countries, I suppose we are well off.

Pat Daniels, Mike Murphy and Neil Hutchings are all young hopefuls who could emerge this season, but a player who could emerge from the shadows is Swansea's Alan Meredith. Meredith is in the mould of Gareth Davies, a tactician, with a calculating brain capable of playing equally well going left or right — but, most importantly, he has a delicate side to his play. He is able to use the ball to send players easily through gaps. Although mid-field in Welsh Rugby generally is full of charging thorough-

breds, it is refreshing to see someone like Meredith who can sit back from it all, and assess the play before taking the necessary action. Cardiff have Gareth Davies, Swansea have Alan Meredith and also Alan Donovan (so unlucky on the Australian tour). It is no coincidence that both these teams played some of the most positive and exciting Rugby in Wales last season. I wonder sometimes if coaches spend sufficient time with the backs, for, as we've seen so often, a dominant pack holding a mortgage on possession cannot do without backs to turn possession into points.

Have we spent too much time in per-

... not even a desperate effort by Tomes can prevent Quinnell's moment of glory.

fecting ways in which to earn quality possession and forgotten how to go about using all this ball?

Having watched a cross-section of rugby over the last four or five years, the onus has been on the three-quarters to be virtually a secondary force, supporting the forwards and not being the striking force. When the All Blacks did this with such devastating effect and with such clinical precision in the sixties, there were cries of ten man rugby . . . I wonder if much of our rugby is geared to that same pattern today?

I hear comments too often after games about a three quarter's ability to make the ball available or about a player chasing and contesting everything. These *are* important factors and at the highest level they can mean the difference between winning and losing, but surely, they should not be the 'norm'. It would be dangerous to allow young players to forget basic and natural techniques, for the feint, swerve or side-step will stand up in any era and their use should be encouraged. Welsh rugby has been well served by them so far — but those moments are becoming less frequent. Wales must not allow the level of skill and ingenuity to drop, even if we are winning Triple Crowns and Grand Slams, for with the prospect of the value of penalties and drop-goals being reduced to two points in the near future, the art of creating and scoring tries will again be all important. Statistics prove that to be totally reliant on physical play

Martin looking for the ball.

Jeff Squire takes on Horton and Scott.

is not the most rewarding way — skill, vision and that indefinable quality (or genius) that is inherent in great players, must be allowed to play their part.

Whilst Bennett is the 'jack-in-the box' runner, prodigious kicker, full of the unorthodox play that can set any stadium alight, Davies is a more calculating performer, with a *complete* range of talents capable of bringing out the best in those around him.

There is no doubt that he grabbed his chance in Australia, where his cool judgement under very difficult circumstances were admired and applauded. His tour performances have created another headache for the Welsh Selectors. They pose the old and familiar problem of contrasting fly-halves. Indeed, they indicated a few years ago that they *are* prepared to act: when Bennett was sensationally dropped in favour of John Bevan. Even though injury upset their plans on that occasion, it was clear that the Selectors were concerned at the lack of fluidity in the back division. Now that Davies has shown in Australia that he can get his three quarter line moving forward at speed creating opportunities for World Class wings, it is very much an open race — when early season form will prove decisive. Will Davies or Bennett face the All Blacks?

Whatever the outcome, one thing is certain, Davies will eventually succeed

Bennett and is destined, as far as I'm concerned, for a long run in the Welsh team. He plays the game, which in my opinion, is best suited to take full advantage of the present-day laws, which allows the pivot extra time and space in which to operate. Many people, including qualified coaches, believe this is an ideal tactic — but it has been the downfall of many fine and gifted players. I naturally applaud the changes in the laws in recent years for they have assisted greatly in making rugby a real spectacle; but it has also meant the changing of certain rôles — particularly that of the fly-half.

12 The Varsity Game

PETER ROBBINS

Not only is the Varsity match one of the oldest fixtures it also occupies, even still and despite the drop in standards, a unique place in the rugby calendar. Both Universities used to provide a regular supply of undergraduate internationals and this was still true until the mid sixties. I exempt the established players such as Tommy Bedford and Chris Laidlaw who came up as fully fledged Internationals.

Of course Varsity match day is still a great social occasion, a sort of winter Wimbledon with identical eating and behavioural rituals. The car parks become a gastronomic centre, but more importantly they become an arena for the mixing of the generations and the rival camps. Part of the joy of an occasion in which you played a leading rôle is in the nostalgic recollection with those who shared your days with you. That seems to me to apply universally to rugby as a game but perhaps more supremely to the Varsity match.

I went up in 1954 and it was most fortunate that there were 10 vacancies in the University 15. I had played for the R.A.F. once and in all honesty had no pretensions to the coveted Blue. Perhaps it is the passage of time that gives one the impression that the Blue is of less value these days, but I recall the tremendous *cachet* of such an honour not only in Oxford but in the world outside.

As things turned out John Currie and I played against Cambridge under the Springbok Captain Paul Johnstone. He

was a truly great player but extremely strict as a captain. The freshmen were in awe of him and curfews were imposed. We lived virtually together in monastic seclusion and I recall one evening at the cinema five of us slipped out for a forbidden but welcome pint. We lost the big match 0-3 and the whole evening was anticlimatic. There were two future test cricketers in that side M.J.K. Smith at full back and J. P. Fellowes-Smith at prop. 'Pom Pom', as Fellows-Smith was known, was a legendary figure at Oxford and the victim of innumerable practical jokes. He once made a break in the opponents' 25 and promptly kicked for touch. He would be found lifting his weighted desk with his neck and anyone who went in during this ceremony would be asked to pile on even more books. An awesome character on the field and he was of course a superb test cricketer.

That Varsity match was really not very entertaining and it had followed an acrimonious affair in 1953. It was time to present the better side of Varsity Rugby and both Universities were fortunate in their choices of captains. We elected Roy Allaway, a liberal South African lawyer with an extraordinary intellectual clairty. Cambridge chose Jeff Clements a man of tremendous character and flamboyance. It was these two who virtually arranged that the 1956 match should be so memorable. It was agreed on a Californian beach that the game should be played in a spirit of adventure and Oxford were blessed by the arrival of

David Brace and M.J.K. Smith at fly half. The rugby world, and Oxford in particular, were able to witness two geniuses in action. Brace was the catalyst with his diagonal running but Smith had the intelligence to interpret his every move. The principle of the Brace/Smith play was that when Brace broke across field other players cut diagonally back never fully knowing whether they would receive the ball or not. This wizardary mesmerised so many teams even though they knew what was going to happen. It always amuses other players in that team to have people ask, "Did you play in the Brace/Smith team?" I and the others always reply, "Yes, and so did twelve other guys."

Oxford won the match 9-5 and it was a marvellous game to play in since, despite an early breakdown of a Brace move, Oxford continued to play in their own style. However, the great lesson for me was in the captaincy. Here was Roy Allaway, an outsider as it were, having the nerve to lay down that we could play risk rugby and still win. There was no thought in his head of not winning but equally there was no thought whatsoever of closing the game up. Also he said that as adults we were free to run our lives as we saw fit with the proviso that if our way of life adversely affected our training or our play then that would put our place in jeopardy.

This enlightened attitude was a great act of faith and it paid off. Indeed some of the pack, though not myself, were so confident on the day that they each had a glass of claret at lunch. Cambridge even thought we were on drugs.

No matter, the important thing was that the Varsity match was restored to its rightful place, and further, that Oxford rugby was again on the up.

David Brace captained the side the following year but was injured for the last part of the term and was forced to play at fly-half in the match. Oxford lost to a good Cambridge side with players such as Marques, Horrocks-Taylor, Windsor-Lewis, Mulligan and Arthur Smith, and the side was captained by a great friend, John Herbert.

1957 was perhaps the happiest year for me personally at Oxford as Captain of the side. Thanks to a marvellous team effort (which the team expected to put in but no one else did), Cambridge were beaten 3-0. It was an unforgettable day and the performances of the players were not lost on national selectors. In fact, that team contained seven present or future internationals and it is true to say that Cambridge had the same number. Ours were predominantly in the pack and that was the key. Yes, they were happy years, hard but blissfully happy. Of course, on the day of my first Varsity match I had had no contact whatsoever with any Cambridge man at all. Tab was someone to hammer hell out of on the day — but combined tours to California, British Columbia, South America, South Africa, Rhodesia, and East Africa mellowed us all and made us friends for life. When it came to the National Anthem in 1957, the dreaded foe but ten yards away, none of us felt the acrimony we had felt perhaps in '54. Those enduring friendships have proved a benefit to sportsmen throughout the world.

There have of course been a variety of humorists over the years. David MacSweeney who went up to Cambridge just prior to drawing his old age pension once told a freshman, "If you win you will be one of the Kings of the Twickenham Ball in that new light blue blazer. If you lose you're just the ice-cream boy." MacSweeney ran for President of the Union without actually being a member and was very nearly elected.

Joe McPartlin was also one of the wits

of the sixties, though as he played, I believe, on four losing sides, it is difficult to know what he found to be funny about. Joe, on his own ommision was a hero at Cardiff — for the Welsh — having dropped a high ball under his post thus allowing Wales to score and win the Triple Crown. He was the only person to broadcast on tour in Africa without the aid of a microphone. It was he that coined the immortal phrase "I have seen better centres in chocolates." Arthur Smith, now sadly no longer with us, coined a beautiful phrase on being asked what he thought of the 1966 Varsity match. He replied "Two poor teams having an off day. There was much less in the match than actually met the eye." My most vivid memory of practical jokes occurred on the way to Cardiff in 1957 when we had a young South African called Dennis Bouwyer who had been in the country only about three weeks. We asked him if he had his passport for the customs to examine or at least a visa from his Embassy. The rest of the team soon latched on to this joke, and Secretary Steven Coles went round picking up a variety of documents purporting to be a visa. I explained meanwhile to Dennis that we had had some trouble the year before with the Welsh customs, having been caught smuggling whisky and that we should hide him in the boot until we had gone through customs.

We stopped five miles outside Chepstow and put him in the boot of the coach. We then paused outside Chepstow and I had a conversation with a Welsh undergraduate who was coming down to the match with us and after perfunctory conversation moved on, being wished good luck by the 'customs officer'. We stopped to open the boot, but there was no sign of Dennis, but we found him hidden in a very large Gladstone bag in which we carried the jerseys.

We kept the joke up all the way, but unfortunately Dennis got injured in the game and had to go to hospital. There took place the most amusing scene, for the nurse said that he might have to stay in hospital over night as he had broken a collar bone.

Dennis loudly and obstinately refused for so long, and was so insistent that she finally asked why he could not stay. Being a very honest man, Dennis came clean and blurted out "Because I haven't got my passport with me." The result was Dennis Bouwyer looking for me all over Oxford on the Sunday.

But what of today? Have standards really fallen and if so why? Why have Cambridge dominated the seventies so conclusively? Well, quite honestly, I really do believe that things are not what they used to be. Firstly, because in the late forties men came back from the war, grown men with obvious advantages. Then, in the fifties, those who went up did so usually after two years' National Service and were consequently older undergraduates and physically stronger to meet the demands of first class rugby. Today that is not the case, it is not the point of this article to discuss the *pros* and *cons*, merely to state reasons. One further disadvantage of the University teams is that club sides are by and large so much better prepared these days and so much better coached. Therefore the traditional gap between fitness and preparation has not only narrowed but it has closed completely. Good big ones will always beat good little ones.

There has also been a tremendous change in the entry policy of sportsmen to the University, particularly at Oxford, where the supply of outstanding games players via the Rhodes Scholarship System has virtually dried up altogether. Oxford seem intent on admission by brain power alone. There is no longer a place for the all-rounder. In my time Teddy Hall was called 'a monastic games club' by the *Times* but looking back, St Edmund Hall was a very happy and rounded place to be at.

By contrast, it seems to me that Cambridge have developed their executive search to a fine degree and have set up an especially good Welsh connection. There is, so it appears, still a place for the all-rounder there, although few would argue the principle of meritocracy: the best balanced world is achieved not by exclusivity and intellect alone.

Oxford would benefit from having regional blues committees to look for talent. I believe that no one wants to see University rugby decline so badly. This system of search practises elitism in sport, and why not? For it to succeed the admission tutors would have to be more sympathetic than they are at present.

Whatever the lament, there is simply no denying the great influence that both Universities have had no rugby throughout the years. It·is equally important for outsiders to remember that Varsity match day belongs to the two teams locked, as it were, in a totally private feud. Part of its uniqueness is that there is no other game of rugby in the world where the defensive play is quite as fast.

Every dog has his day, and my word, the production-line of talent emitted by both the Universities is like a rugby Who's-who of pre-and post-war. That supply sadly is drying up, for reasons I have stated. Nevertheless, playing in that match is a unique experience. They have their memories and I hope personally those who follow in the future will have equally happy memories. But more importantly, it is my hope that they will be able to raise the standard that once was typical of both these centres of excellence.

13 "Forget the moves, just give me the ball at speed!" CARWYN JAMES

It is Sunday evening, 11 June, 1978. A few hours ago, in Brisbane, Wales lost the first of two Test matches to Australia by 18 points to 8. Paul McClean kicked 14 points and Wales scored two tries to the Wallabies' one including a record nineteenth for Gerald Davies, who also broke Ken Jones's record of 44 appearances for his country.

A few minutes ago I watched a sad interview on television between West Bromwich Albion's Willie Johnston who admitted to Frank Bough that he had taken a couple of tablets prescribed by his family doctor because on the day Scotland played Peru he had a cold and felt low. The taking of drugs or pep pills will now be a major issue. No doubt the F.A. will set up an enquiry. Rugger, the R.F.U. will tell us, is above this kind of thing.

In today's *Telegraph,* Tony Lewis has an article to which a sub-editor has given the title: 'Heading for state of faceless men', the head without a face which is protected by a crash-helmet type headgear. The ultimate in the comic or farcical situation is seeing these helmeted batsmen playing the leggie or the off-spinner.

The sadness of cricket in the seventies, much of it of the instant variety, is that we see too little spin and too much pace. The quickies have come into their own and such as Thomson and Lilley have demanded that the international contest is the battle of the bouncers. So many bouncers are being bowled that the authorities have issued statements involving umpires, captains, rabbits and nightwatchmen. The players, on the other hand, have taken the law into their own hands and they have designed protective headgear. Perhaps, in future, for recognition purposes, they will wear a number on their backs.

Willie Johnston (Scotland).

We live in a violent society. If a gentle, languid game for gentlemen like cricket succumbs to violence, and Lords approve, then what chance for the physical contact sports? American Rugby, the intricate 'pro' game ruled by the iron fist of the coach, has always insisted on crash helmets, padded shoulders and thigh pads, boxes to protect the family jewels and the like. What price similar protection in Rugby Football?

My theory very simply is that in Rugby a higher value is placed on the tough, physical, crash-ball, setter-upper of a maul in mid-field than on the player with skill and artistry. What we have seen in recent years is the decline of centre play to an abysmally low level. No longer do we seem able to produce the instinctive player, the touch player. As coaches we have a lot to answer for.

None of us believes in bad coaching. But, in recent years no one can deny that

An American football game between New England and The Jets.

we have tended to play our game by numbers. May I speak from experience as a fly-half for Llanelli in the fifties. I used to be amused when a particular centre would ask me for the ball on the burst even before the ball had been put into the scrum. Absolute nonsense. I didn't know what kind of ball I was going to have. But the common practice today is to call the move before the set-piece takes place, a practice, I must admit, accentuated by law changes.

The result, too often, is a mess and a muddle in mid-field. The crash-ball centre play hides a multitude of sins. All the International teams resort to it, that is, when they are prepared to play an extension of the nine- or the ten-man type of game. In game after game at both international and club level the likes of Gerald Davies are neglected; not only at the first phase but, too often, when quality possession is gained at the second or the third phase.

It is true that law changes, and particularly the laws relating to the off-side line, have nurtured this thinking more than the instinctive players. The pressurised mid-field players of the fifties and the early sixties had to play much of their game by instinct. Now that the back-row forwards are forced to pursue less aggressive angles the fly-half and the centres have more time to think and, amazingly, the quality of centre play in the modern game has deteriorated alarmingly.

I have always thought that quality centres and flankers are interchangeable. At least, that the majority of skilful flankers with footballing sense would make good centres. In the modern game this is more apparent than ever. Gravell, Milliken, Bergiers, Kent and others would make excellent flankers. The problem is that they are asked to play a flanker type game in the centre. They are used as battering rams either to pene-trate fragile defences by force or they are asked in the manner of Ian Macrae to take a centre or two out of the game in order to set up the maul or the ruck.

The problem is that this type of game becomes second nature to them. Force takes over from skill. May I take an analogy from cricket? Alec Bedser, in his day as a splendid swing bowler, is concerned that few fast bowlers in the modern game have the ability to swing the ball. They are either unimpressed with the learning of an ancient art or they lose it because they prefer, in this age of violence, to try and intimidate the batsman by bowling as fast as possible at the body and they gain far more pleasure from the bouncers than they do from swinging the ball.

Tony Lewis sums it all up: "Botham bowled poorly in Pakistan's first innings at Edgbaston because he tried to bowl too quickly. The second time around he cut back his speed, pitched the ball farther up and swung it appreciably. He has all the natural gifts of a top-class medium fast bowler as long as he hangs on to the skills."

The intimidation, inevitably, has affected the art of batting. It is breeding a generation of batsmen who are shifting across the crease even before the ball is delivered. The disappearing art of great batsmanship is the steady, balanced, well-poised art of standing still at the crease and playing each ball on its merit. As in Rugby Football decisions are made too soon and in consequence the decision makers have only themselves to blame when they look stupid.

I have never been a great fan of the New Zealand artificial platform type of pattern which Macrae introduced initially and which was subsequently copied by Jaggie Jansen in South Africa and others I have already mentioned in the U.K. We need to re-assess the centre play of Butterfield and Davies or

Bleddyn Williams and Mathews. Davies and Mathews were the hard men of the fifties but first and foremost they were ball distributors who allowed Butterfield and Williams the time and the space to perfect the art of passing. In such company Gerald Davies would have crossed the line for scores of tries for both his club and his country.

Recently I had occasion to speak with two distinguished gentlemen who have contributed much to the game, both of whom have studied its development for some sixty years. Both, and I would agree with them, maintained that the basic pattern for quality back play was to move the ball at maximum speed from scrumhalf to wing threequarter. Sir Wavell Wakefield used the expression, "like molten lead" and Mr. T. P. Williams, the successful coach at Llandovery College for many years, the phrase "like

'Who overcomes by force, hath overcome but half his foe.' — Donovan injured in the Second Test between Australia and Wales.

lightning". I'm afraid that in the modern game this is a luxury that we seldom see. The Australian schoolboys of this year were a glowing exception. What a pity that their elders failed to perceive the beauty of a successful pattern — a pattern which endeared the 1927 Waratahs to British spectators and a pattern which the Wallabies of 1966 spearheaded by Catchpole and Hawthorne left a lasting impression on many of us.

I'm sorry for the up-and-coming centres in our modern game. I have only seen one player of rare quality in the last couple of seasons. His name, Rino Francescato. One of three brothers who plays for Ireviso and for Italy, all three-quarters. He has balance and timing. He has learnt the art of finger-tip passing.

England captain Mike Brearley wearing his crash helmet.

He is already the master of the outside break. In October of last year he made a mockery of the All Blacks defence.

Recently he was playing with a fly-half who, in the modern idiom, was calling the pre-meditated moves before assessing the quality of the ball. Quietly he turned to the fly-half and said: "Forget the moves, just give me the ball at speed." That is the essence of good threequarter play.

Perhaps Milton summed up the modern phenomenon better than most when he said: "Who overcomes by force, hath overcome but half his foe."

Right:
Tony Ward.

14 The All Blacks clean up

CHRIS LAIDLAW

The popular image of just about every All Black team that has rampaged through Britain has been that of a sombre, introverted bunch of perfectionists, dedicated to imposing their corporate personality on each of their British victims.

That obsession with perfectionism has now passed on, itself the victim of a new generation of New Zealand players unprepared to devote themselves as completely to the cause as their predecessors. All Blacks teams are now lighthearted, extrovert and full of fun. And not the kind of sinister fun that forced Keith Murdoch to clobber a Cardiff security guard in 1972 when the pressure to succeed became just too great. Happily, it seems that that trench warfare attitude to touring has now been seen for what it really was — small-minded and reactionary.

It might surprise many British rugby followers to see an All Black team that can let its hair down at the beginning of a tour rather than at the end, against the Barbarians. But that is what they are very likely to see. And, provided the British sporting press can see it that way too — which, knowing their instincts, can never be guaranteed — then the 1978 All Black tour could go a long way to healing some of the wounds originally opened during the 1972/3 tour and rendered gangrenous after the 1977 Lions tour.

But quite apart from the emotional element, the most striking feature of All Black rugby of the late 1970s is its new spirit of adventure in the field. Given the noticeable deterioration in British back play in the last few seasons and the discovery of new breed of really exciting runners in New Zealand we could be faced with the astonishing sight of heavyweight British forward packs and solid but unenterprising backs struggling to contain free-running New Zealanders. Such a sight would prompt many Welshmen into thinking that the world has gone wrong. Things surely shouldn't happen that way.

If anything is certain then it is that the wonderful era of New Zealand forward dominance is over. These days they are pushed about in the scrums, outjumped in the lines out and, most distressing of all, outmauled in the rucks. The new ruling allowing a free hand, so to speak, in rucking is a very definite nail in the coffin of New Zealand rucking tradition. It is surprising that they haven't fought harder to resist this apparently innocuous modification to a law which promises to eliminate clean rucking altogether. One suspects a little bit of trickery at the IRB; but then that's nothing new.

Tears have been seen to accumulate in the eye of Colin Meads as he has watched recent New Zealand forward efforts from the obscurity of the grandstand. The fact is that New Zealand just doesn't have the players to beat anybody in the forwards these days. The 1978 team will only have four or five forwards of true international class, the Captain Graham

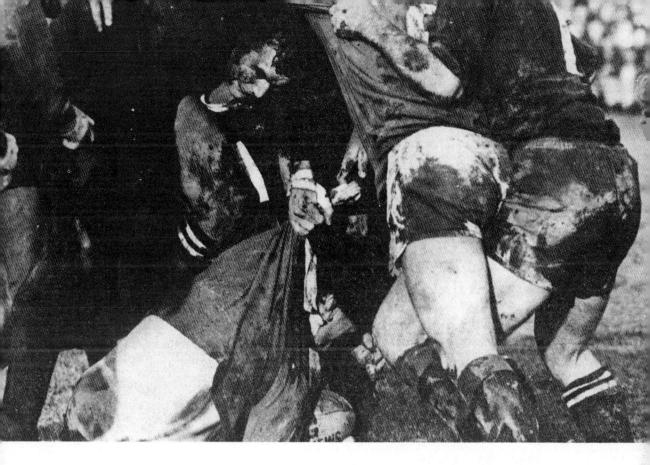

Haden in action against
the 1977 Lions.

Left:
Bryan Williams.

Mourie, Laurie Knight, Gary Sear, Kevin Eveleigh, and Brad Johnston. Significantly, all are loose forwards except Johnstone who is a prop. The rest will be capable — N.Z. forwards always are — but not inspired. Gone are the days when gigantic youngsters came down from the hills and after a year or two were fully seasoned in New Zealand forward play. Today those youngsters have to be coaxed out of offices or company cars to training. The image of the unsmiling giant created by Meads, Gray, Tremain, Lochore and Whineray is just now a myth.

The chief contenders, perhaps better called 'pretenders', to the tight forward succession are Andy Haden, Frank Oliver, Gary Knight, Billy Bush and John Calleson. All of these would be lucky to make a Welsh or English pack (although the Scots or Irish would certainly welcome them). It seems amazing that

despite the ravages of old age such proven figures as Ian Kirkpatrick, Peter Whiting and Ken Stewart, who are thoroughly familiar to British rugby, and all the more valuable for it, should have to remain on the scrapheap. Even Alex Wyllie and Alan Sutherland, old fashioned meanies, would be welcomed back by their comrades although I rather doubt that the Rugby Writers' Association would exhibit quite the same enthusiasm.

Against this gloomy outlook up front, there is positive enthusiasm behind the scrum. Sid Going, after 10 years of coming, is now gone, retired to eternal glory in north Auckland and, no doubt, to the profound relief of many British loose forwards. His successor, if not quite as devastatingly strong, is a better all-round player and not half as predictable. Mark Donaldson, who played outstandingly well against the French behind a pack in

123

wholesale retreat most of the time, seems destined to become the lynch-pin of the New Zealand attack. Comparisons with Gareth Edwards will be tempting but perhaps a little premature. The one advantage Donaldson will definitely have is his speed of pass; in this he is quite clearly better than any other international scrum half of the moment. Kevin Greene, his understudy, is much the same sort of player. Both are tactically clever as they proved against the French last year.

Outside, talent abounds. To the familiar names of Bruce Robertson, Bryan Williams and Doug Brace can be added Mark Taylor and Bill Osborne — two razor sharp centres, even if neither possesses a built-in compass. But the player who may rightly be regarded as the real star is the wing Stuart Wilson. It was he who scored so brilliantly against France last year to seal a truly remarkable All Black victory in Paris against fearsome odds and he has eclipsed Bryan Williams as the current danger-man. Several other exciting wingers are also attracting attention as are the increasing number of all-rounders like Brian McKechnie and yet another Wilson who may be brought along as utility backs, capable of playing at fullback or fly half, or just about anywhere else.

If a major weakness exists it is the quality of the defence that the All Blacks will offer. Many of the emergent youngsters in New Zealand have four forward speeds but, alas, no reverse. This, too, represents a departure from past tradition — tackling being a strong feature of almost every All Black touring team's repertoire. Against crash exponents of the quality of Ray Gravell or Charles Kent the New Zealand backs may be

Billy Bush — a contender for the tight-head position.

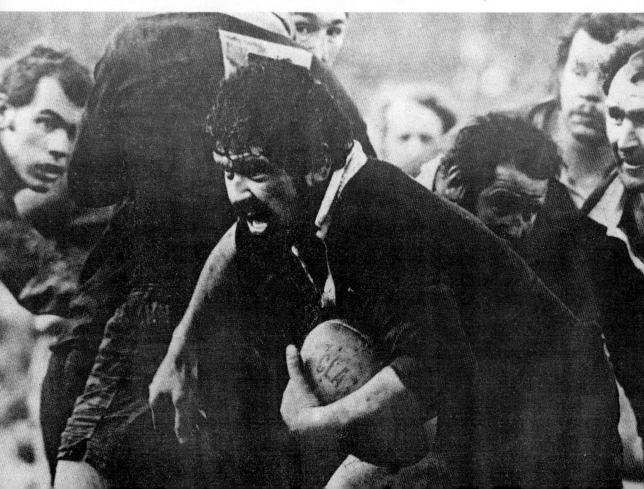

made to look very fragile. Yet the discipline which inevitably flows from constant training, field organisation and co-ordination on a tour will undoubtedly improve the defence. Much in this respect will depend on Doug Bruce, the Canterbury fly half, who is a first class organiser and on the field tactician. He personally devised the clever switches and changes of tactic that so upset the French team in Paris. It was he too that gradually wore down Phil Bennett in the Test Series that the Lions played in New Zealand last year. While Bruce may not have the lightning footwork or sheer speed of Bennett he is a cool, economical player who is now vastly experienced and, having played with the Canterbury team for so long, unaccustomed to losing.

The New Zealanders are once again faced with what seems to be an impossibly difficult itinerary. It must be admitted that Lions teams visiting New Zealand complain, too, that they are given no respite but, in fact, there are always a few easy matches against minor provinces and as provincial rugby gradually weakens there is now considerable opportunity to relax — as the 1977 Lions discovered. The 1978 All Blacks however will, apart perhaps from the university match, have no such opportunities and one wonders why killer itineraries like this are so readily accepted. Not any more a game against, say, Southern Counties, which might be expected to be little better than mediocre. All British regional teams are now strong — particularly in the Midlands and the North. It is inconceivable these days to imagine an

Osborne breaks through.

undefeated run through Britain. Some matches may simply have to be sacrificed. The problem is, which ones?

The British rugby public are not only in for a surprise so far as the New Zealand spirit of adventure is concerned; they will also be treated to the odd sight of occasional two or three main New Zealand scrums, frequent short or quickly executed lines out and complex short penalty manoevres. Most of these tricks have been introduced by Jack Gleeson, the new All Blacks Coach, who has come as something of a revelation to New Zealand rugby. He believes in the same sort of fluid rhythm that Fred Allen introduced years ago but his methods of achieving that are much more unorthodox. Where Allen preached pure flowing fifteen-man rugby the sight of which so inspired British enthusiasts in 1967, Gleeson likes a more frenetic, hustle-bustle style and he has already enjoyed a lot of success, particularly when one considers the shortages of talent in many positions with which he has had to cope.

That the New Zealand players themselves like it too goes without saying. Gleeson is enormously popular with both players and public in New Zealand ever since he sneaked past the more phlegmatic J. J. Stewart in a national vote for Chairman of selectors (which, in the odd logic of the New Zealand system, one must be before becoming national coach).

Needless to say there are many cynics in New Zealand who are waiting for Gleeson to come a thud. Some thought they had him after the All Blacks were towelled by France in the first test match in Toulouse. They had to eat their words after the second.

Equally important to the success of the coming tour will be Gleeson's easy, relaxed approach to people beyond the stadium. He is an intelligent, highly per-ceptive individual, not at all inhibited by the tensions of international rugby as were his more volatile predecessors, Allen and Stewart. Too often in the past, relations, particularly with the local press, have been soured by misunderstandings arising from the arrogance or pigheadedness of the coach of the touring team. Sad as it may seem, John Dawes, the unfortunate coach of successively unsuccessful Lions and Welsh teams, has demonstrated how easily such misunderstandings can arise. Whether coaches, managers or even players like it or not they simply must be prepared to cultivate an agreeable relationship with the press. Without it they can be nailed to the dressing room wall.

The last major tour by the All Blacks to this part of the world was, socially speaking, an out-and-out disaster. The causes of that were many—not the least being the team's obsessive desire to prove itself after being outplayed on its home territory — something which had never before occurred and the memory of which had to be forcibly blotted out.

The world (or that little part of it devoted to rugby) remembers that tour as the very lowest point in rugby relations between Britain and New Zealand. It was the tour of violence which spread beyond the field, culminating in the expulsion of Keith Murdoch, the rogue elephant prop whose will to behave cracked before the taunts of Welsh supporters. It was a tour which set the cause of sane, intelligent rugby back many years. Keith Murdoch was no worse a performer than many other players — among them Britons — who have visited New Zealand. He took the rap for many others and has forever to live with that burden.

Maximum tension is of course always generated when New Zealanders confront Welshmen. The long history of intense rivalry between the two

Right:
Kirkpatrick: on the scrap-heap?

countries is replete with moments of excessive determination to win — unusual for amateur sportsmen — perhaps unrivalled anywhere for its ferocious devotion. New Zealand players are reminded, needlessly, before they leave home that no matter what else a victory over Wales is the only vital element in a tour of Britain and France. And so far they have, with only two falls from grace, come home with that victory. Sometimes the win has rung a little hollowly — 1974 was such an occasion. Never has it been overwhelming; that would be unthinkable. This year it may be beyond the resources of the New Zealanders. Cardiff Arms Park being what it is in emotional value to the Welsh and bearing in mind the extraordinary reserves of strength the Welsh enjoy at present.

Yet the suspicion lingers that perhaps, for the first time in more than fifty years, New Zealand may be capable of winning expansively at Cardiff by running attacks which the Welsh for all their strength on the flanks may not be able to contain in midfield and close to the scrum. That of course may be no more than wishful thinking from someone who has had the special privilege of beating Wales at Cardiff but only as a consequence of a rigid, unexpansive tactical plan (and, I suspect, the Grace of God).

The only really important issue is whether, in an era of severe strain on the amateur approach, players, press, management and spectators can collectively allow themselves the luxury of remembering that the game desperately needs an injection of rationality, understanding and goodwill. Feuding between countries, of the sort which arose during Wales's tour of Australia is not in the end, worth the effort. The 1978 All Black tour should be a golden chance for everybody to put rugby back into its right perspective — so long as the All Blacks win of course.

Left:
Bruce Robertson.

15 Farewell, Gareth and Gerald

CLEM THOMAS

Gareth Edwards is now a legend, one of the great patron saints of Welsh Rugby, elevated not only by a fabulous record of fifty-three consecutive appearances during which he scored a record-breaking twenty tries for Wales, and by contributing massively to three Grand Slams and five Triple Crowns over a period of eleven years; but by his ingenuous charm and gentle modesty.

I cannot recall any bad or boorish behaviour by him either on or off the field whilst he was playing for Cardiff and Wales or touring with the British Lions. In fact he was the model of what one would want one's own son to be: intense, competitive, dedicated, always cheerful and never brash or impolite, even with the most terrifying 'heavy'.

He made both the game of rugby and its ethics a part of his life and when he played for club or country, he played with his heart and soul.

From the War until 1960 I played with or against all the great scrum-halves of that period and since then I have seen them all. I got my first cap under the captaincy of the great Haydn Tanner and while I hate to draw comparisons between different eras, I would take Edwards before Tanner, because of his sustained power and pace.

There were others perhaps as gifted as Gareth in many ways, Ken Catchpole of Australia got the ball away quicker than any scrum-half I ever saw, Sid Going of New Zealand was more aggressive and durable, Chris Laidlaw, also of New Zealand, had as good a pass, and Dawie de Villiers of South Africa was a beautifully instinctive footballer, but I believe that in the end Gareth had it over them all, as since 1974 there was not a weakness in his game, and he had such an armoury of skills that he could produce more firepower than any other scrum-half.

Gareth Edwards acknowledges the ovation for his epic try against Scotland (1972).

When he began playing for Wales there were gaps in his play — his distribution tended to be neurotic, and his temperament was sometimes suspect. However, such was his determination that he gradually strengthened any deficiencies. In the early days Barry John tended to be the senior partner in their partnership, but after Barry's retirement Gareth took on the tactical control of the Lions' play in 1974 and then the Welsh side and it was this control which in my view brought Wales three consecutive and remarkable Triple Crowns.

The departure of Gareth from the game which he graced with such fabulous distinction will leave a gap which we, who were privileged to watch him play, will be fortunate to see filled with such brilliance in our lifetime.

It was his kicking to the diagonals which was the platform which supported many a suspect Welsh pack. He was a scrum-half without a peer in Welsh rugby. He was a man of charm and charisma and there is no better epitaph to his reign than to recall those two jewels of tries in a brilliant career. Firstly, the one he scored for the Barbarians against New Zealand and secondly, the try for his country against Scotland in 1972 which epitomised the magic of his play. Quite simply he was the greatest.

Opposite Top:
Gareth scores against Ireland (1973).

Opposite Bottom:
Gerald Davies scores another 'impossible' try.

Bottom:
Gareth's first game against France.

Left:
Gerald on the 1971
Lions tour.

Gerald Davies was no less unforgettable than Gareth Edwards. The 'Winged Mercury' of Welsh rugby over the last decade, who ran like quicksilver and delighted the senses with his vivacity and audacity.

He too will never be forgotten in the mind's eye for his breathtaking capacity to sink or sear the ground with his electrifying outside bursts. At times one felt he could go through the eye of a needle, such was his capacity for taking limited opportunity.

He holds the record of forty-six caps for a three-quarter and is equal record holder with Gareth Edwards having scored 20 times for Wales.

He was transferred from centre to wing three-quarter on the ill-fated Welsh tour of New Zealand in 1969 and I well remember his reluctance which bordered on annoyance at being pressed into service on the wing. However, his play has not been affected in any way, and he even bettered his own high standards. His devastating running in the first-half of the second test was something I shall never forget even though Wales lost badly. That day a great star was born which for the next seven years shot across the Welsh firmament with dazzling brilliance.

Just like his great comrade in arms, Gareth Edwards, he too has been an outstanding example of a well-balanced personality who has been a credit to the game which he has adorned with skill, charm and great modesty.

Many will remember him for those four fabulous tries he scored for Cardiff to beat Pontypool in the quarter-final of the Welsh Cup in 1977 and for the hat-trick of tries he scored against Hawkes Bay for the British Lions in 1971.

He too was among the greatest of Welsh backs and like Edwards he will remain as one of the great excitements in our memory of a lifetime of international rugby.

Gerald Davies on his
way to his hat-trick
against Hawkes Bay
(1971).

WELSH TEAM 1977/78

16 The teams and their records

WALES

WALES v. ENGLAND

4th February, 1978 (Twickenham)

Referee: N. Sansom (Scotland)

ENGLAND 6, WALES 9

Wales: *Backs:* J. P. R. Williams; T. G. R. Davies; R. W. Gravell; S. P. Fenwick; J. J. Williams; P. Bennett; G. O. Edwards. *Forwards:* G. Price; R. W. Windsor; A. G. Faulkner; A. J. Martin; G. A. D. Wheel; D. Quinnell; T. J. Cobner; J. Squire.

Scorers: Penalties: P. Bennett (3).

England: *Backs:* A. J. Hignell; P. J. Squires; B. J. Corless; P. Dodge; M. A. C. Slemen; J. P. Horton; M. Young. *Forwards:* B. G. Nelmes; P. J. Wheeler; M. Burton; J. P. Scott; M. J. Rafter; W. B. Beaumont; N. E. Horton; R. J. Mordell.

Scorers: Penalties: A. J. Hignell (2).

WALES v. SCOTLAND

18th February, 1978 (Cardiff Arms Park)

Referee: J. H. West (Ireland)

WALES 22, SCOTLAND 14

Wales: *Backs:* J. P. R. Williams; T. G. R. Davies; R. W. Gravell; S. P. Fenwick; J. J. Williams; P. Bennett; G. O. Edwards. *Forwards:* A. G. Faulkner; R. W. Windsor; G. Price; D. Quinnell; A. J. Martin; G. A. D. Wheel; J. Squire; T. J. Cobner.

Scorers: Tries: G. O. Edwards; S. P. Fenwick; R. W. Gravell; D. Quinnell. Penalty: P. Bennett. Dropped Goal: P. Bennett.

Scotland: *Backs:* B. H. Hay; W. B. B. Gammell; J. M. Renwick; A. G. Cranston; D. Shedden; I. R. McGeechan; D. W. Morgan. *Forwards:* J. McLauchlan; G. T. Deans; N. E. K. Pender; A. J. Tomes; A. F. McHarg; M. A. Biggar; D. S. M. MacDonald; C. B. Hegarty. *Substitute:* G. Hogg for D. Shedden.

Scorers: Tries: J. M. Renwick; A. J. Tomes. Penalties: D. W. Morgan (2).

WALES v. IRELAND

4th March, 1978 (Lansdowne Road, Dublin)

Referee: G. Domercq (France)

IRELAND 16, WALES 20

Wales: *Backs:* J. P. R. Williams; T. G. R. Davies; R. W. Gravell; S. P. Fenwick; J. J. Williams; P. Bennett; G. O. Edwards. *Forwards:* G. Price; R. W. Windsor; A. G. Faulkner; D. Quinnell; T. J. Cobner; A. J. Martin; G. A. D. Wheel; J. Squire.

Scorers: Tries: S. P. Fenwick Fenwick; J. J. Williams. Penalties: S. P. Fenwick (4).

Ireland: *Backs:* A. H. Ensor; C. M. H. Gibson; A. R. McKibbin; P. McNaughton; A. C. McLennan; A. J. Ward; J. J. Moloney. *Forwards:* P. A. Orr; P. C. Whelan; E. Byrne; W. P. Duggan; S. A. McKinney; M. I. Keane; R. W. Steele; J. F. Slattery;.

Scorers: Try: J. J. Moloney. Dropped Goal: A. J. Ward. Penalties: A. J. Ward (3).

WALES v. FRANCE

18th March, 1978 (Cardiff Arms Park)

Referee: A. Welsby (England)

WALES 16, FRANCE 7

Wales: *Backs:* J. P. R. Williams; G. Evans; R. W. Gravell; S. P. Fenwick; J. J. Williams; P. Bennett; G. O. Edwards. *Forwards:* A. G. Faulkner; R. W. Windsor; G. Price; A. J. Martin; G. A. D. Wheel; J. Squire; D. Quinnell; T. J. Cobner.

Scorers: Tries: P. Bennett (2). Conversion: P. Bennett. Dropped Goals: G. O. Edwards; S. P. Fenwick.

France: *Backs:* J. M. Aguirre; G. Noves; R. Bertranne; C. Belascain; D. Bustaffa; B. Vivies; J. J. Gallion. *Forwards:* R. Paparemborde; G. Cholley; A. Paco; F. Haget; M. Palmie; J. P. Rives; J. C. Skrela; J. P. Bastiat.

Scorers: Try: J. P. Skrela. Dropped Goal: B. Vivies.

FRANCE

FRANCE v. ENGLAND

21st January, 1978 (Parc des Princes, Paris)

Referee: N. Sansom (Scotland)

FRANCE 15, ENGLAND 6

France: *Backs:* J. M. Aguirre; J. F. Gourdon; R. Bertranne; C. Belascain; J. L. Averous; B. Vivies; J. J. Gallion. *Forwards:* R. Paparemborde; A. Paco; G. Cholley; J. P. Bastiat; J. C. Skrela; M. Palmie; J. F. Imbernon; J. P. Rives.

Scorers: Tries: R. Bertranne; J. J. Gallion. Conversions: J. M. Aguirre (2). Penalty: J. M. Aguirre.

England: *Backs:* D. Hare; P. J. Squires; B. J. Corless; A. Maxwell; M. A. C. Slemen; A. Old; M. Young. *Forwards:* M. Burton; P. J. Wheeler; R. Cowling; J. P. Scott; P. J. Dixon; N. Horton; W. B. Beaumont; M. J. Rafter. *Substitutes:* C. Kent replaced A. Maxwell; A. Neary replaced Dixon.

Scorers: Dropped Goals: A. Old (2).

FRANCE v. SCOTLAND

4th February, 1978 (Murrayfield)

Referee: C. G. P. Thomas (Wales)

SCOTLAND 16, FRANCE 19

France: *Backs:* J. M. Aguirre; J. F. Gourdon; R. Bertranne; C. Belascain; J. L. Averous; B. Vivies; J. J. Gallion. *Forwards:* R. Paparemborde; A. Paco; G. Cholley; J. P. Bastiat; J. C. Skrela; M. Palmie; F. Haget; J. P. Rives.

Scorers: Tries: J. J. Gallion; F. Haget. Conversion: J. M. Aguirre. Penalties: J. M. Aguirre (3).

Scotland: *Backs:* A. R. Irvine; B. H. Hay; J. M. Renwick; I. R. McGeechan; D. Shedden; R. Wilson; D. W. Morgan. *Forwards:* J. McLauchlan; C. T. Deans; N. Pender; A. J. Tomes; A. F. McHarg; M. A. Biggar; G. Y. Mackie; C. B. Hegarty. *Substitutes:* A. G. Cranston for A. R. Irvine; G. Hogg for D. Shedden.

Scorers: Tries: A. R. Irvine; D. Shedden. Conversion: D. W. Morgan. Penalties: D. W. Morgan (2).

FRANCE v. IRELAND

18th February, 1978 (Parc des Princes, Paris)
Referee: C. G. P. Thomas (Wales)
FRANCE 10, IRELAND 9

France: *Backs:* J. M. Aguirre; L. Bilbao; R. Bertranne; C. Belascain; J. L. Averous; B. Vivies; J. J. Gallion. *Forwards:* R. Paparemborde; A. Paco; G. Cholley; J. P. Bastiat; J. C. Skrela; F. Haget; M. Palmie; J. P. Rives.

Scorers: Try: J. J. Gallion. Penalties: J. M. Aguirre (2).

Ireland: *Backs:* A. H. Ensor; C. M. H. Gibson; A. R. McKibbin; P. McNaughton; A. C. McLennan; A. J. Ward; J. J. Moloney. *Forwards:* P. A. Orr; P. C. Whelan; E. Byrne; W. P. Duggan; S. A. McKinney; M. I. Keane; H. W. Steele; J. F. Slattery.

Scorers: Penalties: A. J. Ward (3).

FRANCE v. WALES

18th March, 1978 (Cardiff Arms Park)
Referee: A. Welsby (England)
WALES 16, FRANCE 7

France: *Backs:* J. M. Aguirre; G. Noves; R. Bertranne; C. Belascain; D. Bustaffa; B. Vivies; J. J. Gallion. *Forwards:* R. Paparemborde; G. Cholley; A. Paco; F. Haget; M. Palmie; J. P. Rives; J. C. Skrela; J. P. Bastiat.

Scorers: Try: J. P. Skrela. Dropped Goal: B. Vivies.

Wales: *Backs:* J. P. R. Williams; G. Evans; R. W. Gravell; S. P. Fenwick; J. J. Williams; P. Bennett; G. O. Edwards. *Forwards:* A. G. Faulkner; R. W. Windsor; G. Price; A. J. Martin; G. A. D. Wheel; J. Squire; D. Quinnell; T. J. Cobner.

Scorers: Tries: P. Bennett (2). Conversion: P. Bennett. Dropped Goals: G. O. Edwards; S. P. Fenwick.

ENGLISH TEAM 1977/78

ENGLAND

ENGLAND v. FRANCE

21st January, 1978 (Parc des Princes, Paris)

Referee: N. Sansom (Scotland)

FRANCE 15, ENGLAND 6

England: *Backs:* D. Hare; P. J. Squires; B. J. Corless; A. Maxwell; M. A. C. Slemen; A. Old; M. Young. *Forwards:* M. Burton; P. J. Wheeler; R. Cowling; J. P. Scott; P. J. Dixon; N. Horton; W. B. Beaumont; M. J. Rafter. *Substitutes:* C. Kent replaced A. Maxwell; A. Neary replaced Dixon.

Scorers: Dropped Goals: A. Old (2).

France: *Backs:* J. M. Aguirre; J. F. Gourdon; R. Bertranne; C. Belascain; J. L. Averous; B. Vivies; J. J. Gallion. *Forwards:* R. Paparemborde; A. Paco; G. Cholley; J. P. Bastiat; J. C. Skrela; M. Palmie; J. F. Imbernon; J. P. Rives.

Scorers: Tries: R. Bertranne; J. J. Gallion. Conversions: J. M. Aguirre (2). Penalty: J. M. Aguirre.

ENGLAND v. WALES

4th February, 1978 (Twickenham)

Referee: N. Sansom (Scotland)

ENGLAND 6, WALES 9

England: *Backs:* A. J. Hignell; P. J. Squires; B. J. Corless; P. Dodge; M. A. C. Slemen; J. P. Horton; M. Young. *Forwards:* B. G. Nelmes; P. J. Wheeler; M. Burton; J. P. Scott; M. J. Rafter; W. B. Beaumont; N. E. Horton; R. J. Mordell.

Scorers: Penalties: A. J. Hignell (2).

Wales: *Backs:* J. P. R. Williams; T. G. R. Davies; R. W. Gravell; S. P. Fenwick; J. J. Williams; P. Bennett; G. O. Edwards. *Forwards:* G. Price; R. W. Windsor; A. G. Faulkner; A. J. Martin; G. A. D. Wheel; D. Quinnell; T. J. Cobner; J. Squire.

Scorers: Penalties: P. Bennett (3).

ENGLAND v. SCOTLAND
4th March, 1978 (Murrayfield)
Referee: J. H. West (Ireland)
SCOTLAND 0, ENGLAND 15

England: *Backs:* D. W. N. Caplan; P. J. Squires; B. J. Corless; P. A. Dodge; M. A. C. Slemen; J. P. Horton; M. Young. *Forwards:* B. G. Nelmes; P. J. Wheeler; F. E. Cotton; J. P. Scott; P. J. Dixon; W. B. Beaumont; M. Colclough; M. J. Rafter.

Scorers: Tries: B. G. Nelmes; P. J. Squires. Conversions: M. Young (2). Penalty: P. A. Dodge.

Scotland: *Backs:* A. R. Irvine; W. B. B. Gammell; J. M. Renwick; A. G. Cranston; B. H. Hay; R. Breakey; D. W. Morgan. *Forwards:* J. MacLauchlan; C. T. Deans; N. E. K. Pender; D. Gray; A. J. Tomes; C. B. Hegarty; D. S. M. MacDonald; M. A. Biggar.

ENGLAND v. IRELAND
18th March, 1978 (Twickenham)
Referee: J. F. Palmade (France)
ENGLAND 15, IRELAND 9

England: *Backs:* D. W. N. Caplan; P. J. Squires; B. J. Corless; P. A. Dodge; M. A. C. Slemen; J. P. Horton; M. Young. *Forwards:* B. G. Nelmes; P. J. Wheeler; F. E. Cotton; J. P. Scott; P. J. Dixon; W. B. Beaumont; M. Colclough; M. J. Rafter.

Scorers: Tries: M. A. A. C. Slemen; P. J. Dixon. Conversions: M. Young (2). Penalty: M. Young.

Ireland: *Backs:* A. H. Ensor; C. M. H. Gibson; A. R. McKibbin; P. McNaughton; A. C. McLennan; A. J. Ward; J. J. Moloney. *Forwards:* P. A. Orr; P. C. Whelan; E. Byrne; W. P. Duggan; R. W. Steele; M. I. Keene; S. A. McKinney; J. F. Slattery.

Scorers: Dropped Goal: A. J. Ward. Penalties: A. J. Ward (2).

IRISH TEAM 1977/78

IRELAND

IRELAND v. SCOTLAND

21st January, 1978 (Lansdowne Road, Dublin)
Referee: P. E. Hughes (England)
IRELAND 12, SCOTLAND 9

Ireland: *Backs:* A. H. Ensor; T. O. Grace; A. R. McKibbin; P. McNaughton; A. C. McLennan; A. J. Ward; J. J. Moloney. *Forwards:* P. A. Orr; P. C. Whelan; M. Fitzpatrick; W. P. Duggan; S. A. McKinney; M. I. Keane; D. Spring; J. F. Slattery. *Substitutes:* L. Moloney for A. H. Ensor; J. O'Driscoll for D. Spring.

Scorers: Try: S. McKinney. Conversion: A. J. Ward. Penalties: A. J. Ward (2).

Scotland: *Backs:* B. H. Hay; A. R. Irvine; J. M. Renwick; I. R. McGeechan; D. Sheddon; R. Wilson; D. W. Morgan. *Forwards:* J. McLauchlan; D. F. Madsen; A. B. Carmichael; D. S. M. MacDonald; A. Biggar; A. J. Tomes; A. F. McHarg; C. B. Hegarty.

Scorers: Penalties: D. W. Morgan (3).

IRELAND v. FRANCE

18th February, 1978 (Parc des Princes, Paris)
Referee: C. G. P. Thomas (Wales)
FRANCE 10, IRELAND 9

Ireland: *Backs:* A. H. Ensor; C. M. H. Gibson; A. R. McKibbin; P. McNaughton; A. C. McLennan; A. J. Ward; J. J. Moloney. *Forwards:* P. A. Orr; P. C. Whelan; E. Byrne; W. P. Duggan; S. A. McKinney; M. I. Keane; H. W. Steele; J. F. Slattery.

Scorers: Penalties: A. J. Ward (3).

France: *Backs:* J. M. Aguirre; L. Bilbao; R. Bertranne; C. Belascain; J. L. Averous; B. Vivies; J. J. Gallion. *Forwards:* R. Paparemborde; A. Paco; G. Cholley; J. P. Bastiat; J. C. Skrela; F. Haget; M. Palmie; J. P. Rives.

Scorers: Try: J. J. Gallion. Penalties: J. M. Aguirre (2).

IRELAND v. WALES

4th March, 1978 (Lansdowne Road, Dublin)

Referee: G. Domercq (France)

IRELAND 16, WALES 20

Ireland: *Backs:* A. H. Ensor; C. M. H. Gibson; A. R. McKibbin; P. McNaughton; A. C. McLennan; A. J. Ward; J. J. Moloney. *Forwards:* P. A. Orr; P. C. Whelan; E. Byrne; W. P. Duggan; S. A. McKinney; M. I. Keane; R. W. Steele; J. F. Slattery;.

Scorers: Try: J. J. Moloney. Dropped Goal: A. J. Ward. Penalties: A. J. Ward (3).

Wales: *Backs:* J. P. R. Williams; T. G. R. Davies; R. W. Gravell; S. P. Fenwick; J. J. Williams; P. Bennett; G. O. Edwards. *Forwards:* G. Price; R. W. Windsor; A. G. Faulkner; D. Quinnell; T. J. Cobner; A. J. Martin; G. A. D. Wheel; J. Squire.

Scorers: Tries: S. P. Fenwick Fenwick; J. J. Williams. Penalties: S. P. Fenwick (4).

IRELAND v. ENGLAND

18th March, 1978 (Twickenham)

Referee: J. F. Palmade (France)

ENGLAND 15, IRELAND 9

Ireland: *Backs:* A. H. Ensor; C. M. H. Gibson; A. R. McKibbin; P. McNaughton; A. C. McLennan; A. J. Ward; J. J. Moloney. *Forwards:* P. A. Orr; P. C. Whelan; E. Byrne; W. P. Duggan; R. W. Steele; M. I. Keene; S. A. McKinney; J. F. Slattery.

Scorers: Dropped Goal: A. J. Ward. Penalties: A. J. Ward (2).

England: *Backs:* D. W. N. Caplan; P. J. Squires; B. J. Corless; P. A. Dodge; M. A. C. Slemen; J. P. Horton; M. Young. *Forwards:* B. G. Nelmes; P. J. Wheeler; F. E. Cotton; J. P. Scott; P. J. Dixon; W. B. Beaumont; M. Colclough; M. J. Rafter.

Scorers: Tries: M. A. A. C. Slemen; P. J. Dixon. Conversions: M. Young (2). Penalty: M. Young.

SCOTTISH TEAM 1977/78

SCOTLAND

SCOTLAND v. IRELAND
21st January, 1978 (Lansdowne Road, Dublin)
Referee: P. E. Hughes (England)
IRELAND 12, SCOTLAND 9

Scotland: *Backs:* B. H. Hay; A. R. Irvine; J. M. Renwick; I. R. McGeechan; D. Shedden; R. Wilson; D. W. Morgan. *Forwards:* J. McLauchlan; D. F. Madsen; A. B. Carmichael; D. S. M. MacDonald; A. Biggar; A. J. Tomes; A. F. McHarg; C. B. Hegarty.

Scorers: Penalties: D. W. Morgan (3).

Ireland: *Backs:* A. H. Ensor; T. O. Grace; A. R. McKibbin; P. McNaughton; A. C. McLennan; A. J. Ward; J. J. Moloney. *Forwards:* P. A. Orr; P. C. Whelan; M. Fitzpatrick; W. P. Duggan; S. A. McKinney; M. I. Keane; D. Spring; J. F. Slattery. *Substitutes:* L. Moloney for A. H. Ensor; J. O'Driscoll for D. Spring.

Scorers: Try: S. McKinney. Conversion: A. J. Ward. Penalties: A. J. Ward (2).

SCOTLAND v. FRANCE
4th February, 1978 (Murrayfield)
Referee: C. G. P. Thomas (Wales)
SCOTLAND 16, FRANCE 19

Scotland: *Backs:* A. R. Irvine; B. H. Hay; J. M. Renwick; I. R. McGeechan; D. Shedden; R. Wilson; D. W. Morgan. *Forwards:* J. McLauchlan; C. T. Deans; N. Pender; A. J. Tomes; A. F. McHarg; M. A. Biggar; G. Y. Mackie; C. B. Hegarty. *Substitutes:* A. G. Cranston for A. R. Irvine; G. Hogg for D. Shedden.

Scorers: Tries: A. R. Irvine; D. Shedden. Conversion: D. W. Morgan. Penalties: D. W. Morgan (2).

France: *Backs:* J. M. Aguirre; J. F. Gourdon; R. Bertranne; C. Belascain; J. L. Averous; B. Vivies; J. J. Gallion. *Forwards:* R. Paparemborde; A. Paco; G. Cholley; J. P. Bastiat; J. C. Skrela; M. Palmie; F. Haget; J. P. Rives.

Scorers: Tries: J. J. Gallion; F. Haget. Conversion: J. M. Aguirre. Penalties: J. M. Aguirre (3).

SCOTLAND v. WALES

18th February, 1978 (Cardiff Arms Park)

Referee: J. H. West (Ireland)

WALES 22, SCOTLAND 14

Scotland: *Backs:* B. H. Hay; W. B. B. Gammell; J. M. Renwick; A. G. Cranston; D. Shedden; I. R. McGeechan; D. W. Morgan. *Forwards:* J. McLauchlan; G. T. Deans; N. E. K. Pender; A. J. Tomes; A. F. McHarg; M. A. Biggar; D. S. M. MacDonald; C. B. Hegarty. *Substitute:* G. Hogg for D. Shedden.

Scorers: Tries: J. M. Renwick; A. J. Tomes. Penalties: D. W. Morgan (2).

Wales: *Backs:* J. P. R. Williams; T. G. R. Davies; R. W. Gravell; S. P. Fenwick; J. J. Williams; P. Bennett; G. O. Edwards. *Forwards:* A. G. Faulkner; R. W. Windsor; G. Price; D. Quinnell; A. J. Martin; G. A. D. Wheel; J. Squire; T. J. Cobner.

Scorers: Tries: G. O. Edwards; S. P. Fenwick; R. W. Gravell; D. Quinnell. Penalty: P. Bennett. Dropped Goal: P. Bennett.

SCOTLAND v. ENGLAND

4th March, 1978 (Murrayfield)

Referee: J. H. West (Ireland)

SCOTLAND 0, ENGLAND 15

Scotland: *Backs:* A. R. Irvine; W. B. B. Gammell; J. M. Renwick; A. G. Cranston; B. H. Hay; R. Breakey; D. W. Morgan. *Forwards:* J. MacLauchlan; C. T. Deans; N. E. K. Pender; D. Gray; A. J. Tomes; C. B. Hegarty; D. S. M. MacDonald; M. A. Biggar.

England: *Backs:* D. W. N. Caplan; P. J. Squires; B. J. Corless; P. A. Dodge; M. A. C. Slemen; J. P. Horton; M. Young. *Forwards:* B. G. Nelmes; P. J. Wheeler; F. E. Cotton; J. P. Scott; P. J. Dixon; W. B. Beaumont; M. Colclough; M. J. Rafter.

Scorers: Tries: B. G. Nelmes; P. J. Squires. Conversions: M. Young (2). Penalty: P. A. Dodge.

HOME INTERNATIONAL CHAMPIONSHIP TABLE 1977/78

	W	D	L	F	A	Pts
WALES	4	0	0	67	43	8
FRANCE	3	0	1	51	47	6
ENGLAND	2	0	2	42	33	4
IRELAND	1	0	3	46	54	2
SCOTLAND	0	0	4	39	68	0

TOP INTERNATIONAL SCORERS 1977/78

WALES

	T	C	P	DG	Total
P. BENNETT	2	1	4	1	25
S. M. FENWICK	2	0	4	1	23
G. O. EDWARDS	1	0	0	1	8

FRANCE

	T	C	P	DG	Total
J. M. AGUIRRE	0	3	6	0	24
J. J. GALLION	3	0	0	0	12
R. BETRANNE	1	0	0	0	4
F. HAGET	1	0	0	0	4
J. P. SKRELA	1	0	0	0	4
B. VIVIES	1	0	0	0	4

ENGLAND

	T	C	P	DG	Total
M. YOUNG	0	4	1	0	11
A. J. HIGNELL	0	0	2	0	6
A. OLD	0	0	0	2	6

IRELAND

	T	C	P	DG	Total
A. J. WARD	0	1	10	2	38*
S. A. McKINNEY	1	0	0	0	4
J. J. MOLONEY	1	0	0	0	4

SCOTLAND

	T	C	P	DG	Total
D. W. MORGAN	0	1	6	0	20
A. R. IRVINE	1	0	0	0	4
J. M. RENWICK	1	0	0	0	4
D. SHEDDEN	1	0	0	0	4
A. J. TOMES	1	0	0	0	4

* This equals the highest individual score for an International Season, held jointly by P. Bennett for Wales and Roger Hisen for England.

WELSH TOUR OF AUSTRALIA 1978

1st Test
AUSTRALIA 18, WALES 8

Wales Scorers: Tries: Gerald Davies; Brynmor Williams.

Australian Scorers: Try: Phil Crow. Penalties: Paul Maclane (4). Conversion: Paul Maclane.

2nd Test
AUSTRALIA 19, WALES 17

Wales Scorers: Tries: Gerald Davies; Terry Holmes. Drop Goal: Gareth Davies. Penalties: Gareth Davies (2).

Australian Scorers: Try: Mark Loame. Penalties: Paul Maclane (3). Drop Goals: Paul Maclane; Laurrie Monahan.

AUSTRALIAN TOUR OF NEW ZEALAND 1978

1st Test
NEW ZEALAND 13, AUSTRALIA 12

New Zealand Scorers: Try: B. Williams. Penalties: B. Wilson (3).

Australian Scorers: Try: Batch. Conversion: K. Wright. Penalties: K. Wright (2).

2nd Test
NEW ZEALAND 22, AUSTRALIA 6

New Zealand Scorers: Tries: M. Taylor; G. Seear; S. Wilson. Conversions: B. Wilson (2). Dropped Goal: D. Bruce. Penalty: B. Wilson.

Australian Scorers: Drop Goal: K. Wright. Penalty: K. Wright.

3rd Test
NEW ZEALAND 16, AUSTRALIA 30

New Zealand Scorers: Tries: J. Ashworth; B. Wilson. Conversion: B. McKechnie. Penalties: B. McKechnie (2).

Australian Scorers: Tries: G. Cornelson (4); G. Pierce. Conversions: T. Melrose; K. Wright. Dropped Goal: T. Melrose. Penalty: K. Wright.

THE ALL BLACKS TOUR OF GREAT BRITAIN 1978

October
18 v. Cambridge University
21 v. Cardiff
25 v. West Wales
28 v. London Counties
31 v. Munster

November
4   v. IRELAND
7   v. Ulster
11 v. WALES
15 v. South and South West
18 v. Midlands
25 v. ENGLAND
29 v. Monmouthshire

December
2   v. North
5   v. Scottish North and
        Midlands
9   v. SCOTLAND
13 v. Bridgend
16 v. BARBARIANS

THE ALL BLACKS TOURING PARTY

Backs: Bevan Wilson (Otago), Clive Currie (Canterbury), Bryan Williams (Auckland), Brian Ford (Marlborough), Stuart Wilson (Wellington), Robert Kururangi (Counties), Bruce Robertson (Counties), Bill Osborne (Wanganui), Lyn Jaffray (Otago), Mark Taylor (Bay of Plenty), Doug Bruce (Canterbury), Eddie Dunn (North Auckland), Mark Donaldson (Manawatu), David Loveridge (Taranaki).

Forwards: Bill Bush (Canterbury), Rod Ketels (Counties), Gary Knight (Manawatu), Brad Johnstone (Auckland), Andy Haden (Auckland), Frank Oliver (Otago), John Loveday (Manawatu), John Fleming (Wellington), Barry Ashworth (Auckland), Leicester Rutledge (Southland), Wayne Graham (Otago), Graham Mourie (Taranaki), Gary Seear (Otago), Ash McGregor (Southland), Andy Dalton (Counties), John Black (Canterbury).

HOME INTERNATIONAL FIXTURES 1979

January 20   — IRELAND v. FRANCE (Lansdowne Road)
             — SCOTLAND v. WALES (Murrayfield)

February 3   — WALES v. IRELAND (Cardiff Arms Park)
             — ENGLAND v. SCOTLAND (Twickenham)

February 17 — FRANCE v. WALES (Parc des Princes)
             — IRELAND v. ENGLAND (Lansdowne Road)

March 3   — ENGLAND v. FRANCE (Twickenham)
             — SCOTLAND v. IRELAND (Murrayfield)

March 17   — WALES v. ENGLAND (Cardiff Arms Park)
             — FRANCE v. SCOTLAND (Parc des Princes)